SIFT

Untitled, Hellmut Sail, Makarska, 1937

S I F T

Memories of childhood

Lawrence Sail

(Lawrence Sail)

1 December 2010

First Published 2010
by Impress Books Ltd
Innovation Centre, Rennes Drive,
University of Exeter Campus, Exeter EX4 4RN

Typeset in 10/13 Palatino by Swales & Willis Ltd, Exeter, Devon

Printed and bound in England by Short Run Press Ltd, Exeter, Devon

British Library Cataloguing in Publication Data
A catalogue record for this book is available from the British Library

ISBN: 978 1 907605 00 0

For Trinny

ACKNOWLEDGEMENTS

I would like to thank Kevin Crossley-Holland, Helen Dunmore, Elizabeth Garrett, Penelope Lively and Erica Sail for their encouragement; Amata Perkins; Martin Sorrell; Colin Morgan, Richard Willis and Julie Swales of Impress Books; and Peter and Greta Williamson for their generosity in making Railford Mill available to me.

The extract from Hermann Hesse's *Siddhartha* is included by kind permission of Suhrkamp Verlag, Berlin, and Peter Owen Publishers, London; and that from Jeremy Harding's *Mother Country* by kind permission of the author, Faber & Faber Ltd and Rogers, Coleridge & White Ltd.

L. S.

'… we suffer the illusion that time is something real.'
HERMANN HESSE, *Siddhartha*
translated by Hilda Rosner

'What are we to say to the dead? That we might have loved them better?'
JEREMY HARDING, *Mother Country*

The birthday party was something of a strain from the start, because of the sheer excitement and because my mother wasn't in the habit of laying on such an event. It became downright bewildering when, along with our guests (most of them seven-year-olds, as we had just become), my sister and I were ushered into a room which had a whole lot of grainy photographs pinned up round the walls. We were all issued with a pencil and a printed card. We were told that we had to guess the subject of each picture; and we mustn't let anyone else see our answers. Apparently they were pictures of quite ordinary things, but we might not recognise them at once. The first to produce a correctly completed card would win a prize.

To begin with, most people stood around for a bit, though one or two rushed over and began looking at the pictures closely. When the rest of us followed suit, we saw that they really were odd. One showed a sort of blobby circle with, somewhere behind it, a dark stubby line going across; another had a straight line in front of a kind of wall in the background; a third appeared to be just a lot of small waves going into the distance. It was a bit like a school test, but quite interesting too. I don't know who won, but it wasn't my sister or me. When we were told the answers, they seemed obvious: a hammer, a cup, a pair of nutcrackers that had been opened out.

I was quite glad when it was time for other games, such as musical chairs. You got hot and bumped into people a bit, which was fun. But when it was all over, and I was lying in bed that night thinking about the party, the game with the photos kept on coming back to me. It intrigued me. I suppose I thought that once you knew the name of a thing you could recognise it for what it was.

Few stories seem to start at their beginning. And what is that, anyway? The striking of an uncle's clock? The exit from Eden, where the angel wields his hot sword? There isn't even agreement about the moment at which life begins. Is it as the sperm docks, burrowing in with a final wriggle suggestive of the consummation that launched it; or with the *whoosh* from the womb into the darkness outside? Or, as the rabbi in an old joke asserts, does life only really begin when the dog has died and the children have left home? By way of evasion, and to adopt the form used by the setters of mathematical problems, let L be the line of the three of us following the road downhill from the station to the town centre, past a row of tall beech trees which marched alongside railings enclosing an open green space. Autumn, and the newly fallen leaves, crisp as Melba toast, lying in generous drifts. Substantial yet light, they were there to kick, to shuffle through, to make as much noise with as possible.

The restraint of the reins held by my mother was irksome at first, as much to my twin sister as me, but we made the best of it, enjoying the alternation of lunging forward and being tugged back. The three of us went on our stuttering way southwards towards the foot of the gradient and a glimpse of the level sea.

No particular feeling attaches to this memory beyond the immediate pleasure of foraging through the brown and brittle piles of leaves, displacing them with a satisfying soughing as we went.

3

We were in the peaceable Devon resort of Sidmouth, and the autumn belonged to 1946. On my mother's side there were already strong family connections with the town. At the age of seven her elder brother Basil had been taken by his granny to the local cinema, the Radway, and was so enchanted that he resolved there and then to become a film-maker, as indeed he did. Her uncle Harold had kept a sailing dinghy there, the *Cockbird*, and did much to promote the welfare of the town's fishermen. A distinguished career as a Liberal, a pacifist and a social activist, marked by his friendship with Norman Angell and his deputy editorship of *The Nation*, was cut short by the ill-health which had dogged him from early childhood, preventing him from attending school and finally overwhelming him at the age of fifty. Both Harold and his father, Charles, were buried in the municipal cemetery. Charles, a confirmed atheist (so to speak), had died only six years earlier, and now rested in the lee of a considerable block of granite. The inscription on it began with what was, perhaps, a defiant response to the Plymouth Brethren persuasion of his parents: *I fall asleep in the full and certain hope that my slumber shall not be broken.*

What had brought my mother to Sidmouth now, however, was the breakdown of her marriage. After we had walked along the front and through the town centre, we would go back to a boarding house somewhere in the hinterland. This is where we had landed up, after an initial flight to a friend of my mother's in Southborough, from the small farm west of Exeter where my parents had been living.

My mother, my parents – just referring to them in one way rather than another can produce complications, or misleadingly suggest the nature or limits of the relationship. And then, Mother, Mummy, Mum, Ma, like a Latin conjugation gone wrong. It's just as bad with father. Father, Daddy, Dad, Pa. Our father, which art somewhere or other. Twins complicate the situation still more: my mother, her father, our parents. For the time before my and my twin sister's birth, I shall generally call them by their forenames, Barbara and Hellmut. Otherwise, at the risk of sounding twee, it will be Mummy and Daddy, simply because that is what, unselfconsciously, we always called them.

*

Apart from the autumnal leaves, my only recollection of the time at Sidmouth centres round a minder of some kind, brought in daily to supervise my sister, Catriona, and myself. 'Nanny' she was called, but this was altogether too grand. Neither of us liked her much, and she hardly improved her standing with us by her habit of pouncing with a fork, quick as a heron, to jab and remove bits of food from our plates. 'You don't want that, do you?' she would ask rhetorically as she struck. Sausages were a favourite. Then one day, and just as abruptly as the pronged food, she was gone. Apparently she had stolen some handkerchiefs from a drawer, a misdemeanour deemed sufficient to warrant dismissal, though this may just have been an excuse.

We cannot have stayed in Sidmouth more than a few months. By the end of the year we had moved into a gangling house on the north side of Exeter, thanks to a modest family trust which would actually own the property. Number 24 Union Road (at four, we were too young to appreciate the irony of the road name, let alone the nuclear family implied by the number) was one in a row of detached and semi-detached brick houses. They varied in height and design. Several, like ours, had white brickwork deployed decoratively round the windows or halfway up, like layers of vanilla icing on a cake: an effect mildly imposing but not beautiful. Most had a small garden in front, and at the rear a long, narrow strip of land running down to a back gate in a wall.

Number 24 loomed skyward behind a quite low wall coated with grey pebbledash. Small pillars rose from the wall at intervals, linked by tubular iron bars, also painted grey. Two cherry trees with papery blossom easily scattered by the wind flanked a small wrought iron gate, at the beginning of a path leading to the front door steps. Beyond a patch of grass, iron railings protected a dark basement area where leaves and litter accumulated. To the left of the house as you looked at it an earth path led down to the back garden: to the right, behind a larger wrought iron gate, was a concrete yard in front of a small garage. The front garden also had a small fuchsia bush and two hydrangeas, one pink and one pale blue, which Mummy disliked but never removed.

On the other side of the road there was land still undeveloped at the time of our arrival, along with a nursery garden next to almshouses belonging to the Licensed Victuallers' Association. Further along Union Road, which ran east and west about halfway up the hill of Pennsylvania, the houses were terraced. There was a corner shop and, opposite it, the Victoria Arms. A small private girls' school stood at the junction with Pennsylvania Road. In the other direction the road became a bit more varied and spacious, with a bowling green and tennis courts, before ending at a roundabout at the foot of Stoke Hill. A strange mixture of a road, dominated by brick and, until rather more costly houses were built on its northern side, considerably closer to modest living than affluence: only one parked car, black, was to be seen the length of it.

Many more people must have lived in the street than you ever saw out.

The house had been built around 1870, though from the look of it you might have guessed a later date. It was L-shaped, with four flights of stairs totalling forty-eight steps (I would count them obsessively, always making sure to end with the left foot leading after I had reached the top or bottom of a flight). Since the house was on a slope, the bottom floor was a basement at the front – the kitchen, with a sizeable larder off it – and level with the garden at the back. Here was the dining-room, and a narrow, dark passage leading to a back door.

The three floors above each had two main rooms, the front ones facing north, the back ones south. On the first floor, a study and a drawing-room; above, the spare room and Mummy's bedroom; and on the top floor, my room next to an additional narrow bedroom, and my sister's room.

At the base of the L was a large room which might once have served as an office. When we moved in, its sole furnishing was a bulky telephone switchboard in one corner, housed in a rather fine mahogany casing. This room, along with the small space with a sink and a stove to the rear of it, continued to be known as the office. Flat-roofed, it was attached awkwardly to the rest of the house and at a slightly different level, necessitating hiccoughs of connecting steps. Externally, it had its own flight of stone steps. It sat on top of three poky sheds, cellars really, accessible only from the back of the house and known collectively as 'down under': our own Australia. In its bareness, mitigated in time by the installation of a ping-pong table, the office had the look of a space waiting for something to be staged in it.

My sister's bedroom commanded an enviable view south-ward over the back garden and rows of houses with similar

7

long narrow gardens, across to the Southern Region railway, deep in its cutting, and St James's Park, the football ground belonging to Exeter City, of the Third Division (South). On home match days you could make out the miniature figures of the teams and get some idea of what was going on, as play moved from one side or end of the pitch to the other. If it was windless, further clues floated over in the tidal responses of the crowd, something between a low roar and a sigh. Occasionally you could even make out a wispy blue trail of pipe and cigarette smoke drifting up from the terraces. Visible beyond the football ground were the hills to the south of the city.

Closer to, from the small conservatory leaning against the dining-room wall the garden sloped downhill, devolving into wildness. After a neat square of lawn, with rickety little arches of climbing roses on three sides, came steps down through a small rockery bright in due season with stonecrop, thrift, mimosa, forget-me-nots, primroses and pinks. When shifted, the lumps of rock themselves, knuckled and white, would thrillingly reveal repellant grey lozenges with legs, swarming about.

Then, a rectangle arranged as three triangular beds, with borders of house-bricks and narrow cinder paths between them, planted with tulips, snapdragons and headily scented wallflowers. Then, a wilder area with long grass, two apple trees and a pear tree, and two tanks, one rectangular and of galvanised iron, with a tap above it, the other a heavy circular one which caught the rainwater. The pear tree we called 'fatty', as so it was by comparison with the apple trees. It had a convenient wide fork not too far off the ground, and we soon learned to climb up to it.

Beyond, there was a vegetable patch and, after that, a few currant and gooseberry bushes too old to be hugely productive. At the very end, rhubarb, a hummock with couch-grass and bindweed, and a holed enamel bowl turned upside down. This part of the garden smelt sour, with a rankness we associated with decay and the rabbit bones easily dug up there.

Near the conservatory, up against the brick wall which was part of Number 22 next door, was a small cracked tombstone. It had an inscription in memory of Ching, 'a faithful friend'. My sister and I agreed that it almost certainly marked the grave not of a pet, but a murdered child.

The house had not cost a lot to buy, and its relative cheapness was expressed in drawbacks. Among the most obvious was the water system, which successive breakdowns and repairs had rendered increasingly complex, even incomprehensible. Dead geysers and abandoned boilers squatted in various caches: under the basement stairs, in a dining room cupboard, on the dripping wall of the bathroom itself, where there were two geysers side by side, one extinct and one operative. 'Operative' meant a terrifying *bloomp!* of gas as the jets exploded into life, squirting flames sideways through the vents in the scorched casing. Ignition, with its clear potential for destruction, brought an uncomfortable reminder that the bathroom was built out from the side of the house at second floor level, with only two wooden brackets, probably rotting if not yet rotten, by way of visible support. Also in the bathroom was a tap smartly marked DRINKING WATER, which everyone took at its labelled word. The lidless iron tank in the roof which fed it, when drained years later, was found to contain the remains of several unfortunate birds. But no one died, apart from the birds, and who knows what still undiscovered medical benefits might not have accrued from the sludge-tonic of bone, feathers and other integuments? In any case, all these watery problems could be looked at positively. If the house were ravaged by rot or all the mortar shaken out of the bricks by a minor earthquake, it would be unlikely to fall down, the structure held in place by miles of copper and lead piping running up, down, across and along.

The damp and the cold were more immediate threats. In the basement kitchen, where the yellow emulsion flaked from the bricks and a smeary mould bloomed round a window looking onto the blank wall of the area, the condensation on the exposed pipe above the sink stopped dripping only when it froze solid. In the top floor bedrooms ice formed on the inside of the windows for up to three months of the year, and the only warmth to be had came from a black oil stove moved from room to room as needed. Its meagre power seemed to be enhanced by the red glow from its small door and the petals of light projected through its slatted top up onto the ceiling. It generated as much fug as heat, with its reek of paraffin, but was no less welcome for that.

It was warmth, as well as the cupboards housing our toys and books, which made the dining-room a favoured place, since it had a stove that could be kept in overnight. The coke and anthracite it consumed produced a fiery core behind its small doors, and it was often too hot to sit on. Sometimes it was used for drying wet clothes or gloves, when the smell of damp wool would fill the room.

Such was the context in which Mummy was to establish her improbable outpost of Austria, where my sister and myself, who could already be said to have owed our birth to Hitler and our English habitat to Franco, lived as in a dream.

Autumn had given way to winter. Not just any winter, but that of 1947, when snow fell somewhere in England every day from the fourth week of January to mid-March. In the South West, it was the heaviest snowfall since 1891.

I stared out at the snow. It swooped across, driven almost horizontal by a blustering near-gale. If the wind slackened for an instant, the snow would start to turn round and back on itself in a vortex, before reforming and whirling away again in an almost unbroken line. It had begun only an hour or so earlier, but already the coal in its wooden coop behind the house had become a miniature range of drifted alps. In the garden, each plant, each branch, each leaf acquired its precise ghost-shadow, until the snow rose to cloak it altogether. Earlier, a bus had ground past, the snowflakes swarming profusely as they poured through the yellow beams of its headlights. Now, with night setting in, there was no traffic at all, only the untrodden bluish white of the snow keeping the night half at bay, and muffling every sound.

Some time after dark, there came a knock at the door – not the usual front door of the house, but the office. I raced my sister up the stairs. We hardly knew anyone – and who would come round in such weather, unless it was Santa Claus on a supplementary New Year visit? And who would knock at that door, where no one had knocked until now? Releasing the snib on the Yale lock, which I could just reach on tiptoe, I struggled in vain to control the door as it drove against me and forced itself open. To my astonishment I recognised the figure standing there at once, even though his hat was brown and not pointed, his height greater and his moustache much neater than in the book. The unignorable likeness inhered in the force of the wind that whistled about him, flicked and shook the ends of his coat, made him lean forward and clutch onto his hat. This figure bent against the gale, with an uproar of every-which-way snowflakes racing madly through the mantle of the street lamp behind him, was clearly Mr South West Wind Esquire, whose picture I had seen in *The King of the Golden River*, a story read to us by Mummy for the first time quite recently.

The man came in and, with some difficulty, closed the door behind him. By now Mummy had appeared at the far end of the room: my sister stood uncertainly between her and me. 'Barbara,' said the man, in a funny accent, and from the way Mummy responded it was evident that she knew him. He stamped his feet to get the snow off, took off his hat and coat, looked round the bare room without success for somewhere to put them down, then slung the coat over his arm and rummaged in one of its pockets. Out came a paper bag, and out of that two little painted wooden animals, one for each of us children. He showed us how you could make them buckle comically, or wag their tail or ears, by pressing the underside of the round base on which they stood.

From somewhere above, as it seemed, but too soft to be the voice of God issuing from a cloud, and with that strange accent again, came the words 'Call me Wolfy'. And now it was another story I was thinking of.

The first hint of any link between my mother's family and the German-speaking world, and a slight enough one at that, came during the First World War. It involved her grandfather, Charles Wright, a radical Liberal prominent in the world of marine insurance. He eventually became chief accountant at Lloyds, but did not forget his origins as the son of a London butcher who had followed his trade in Maple Street. A beneficiary of the Working Men's College and later its benefactor, he had a natural feeling for those denied opportunities, or on whom society seemed to frown. Unsurprisingly, he had taken up the cause of conscientious objectors, and also concerned himself with the plight of innocent people labelled 'enemy aliens' in Surrey, where he lived. This led to him being sent a short but vehement anonymous letter:

> Dear Sir,
> Beware. In a few days you will be shown up for a hipocritt and a progerman which is what you are as you know ostensible. So beware in time and to honestly confess and oblidge.
>
> X
>
> p.s. You are a worm of hell.

Quite apart from the spelling, there is something almost endearing about the ineffectual rage which the postscript betrays. No doubt the writer would have considered himself (or herself, though this seems somehow unlikely) amply justified by subsequent events, in the form of Mummy's obsession with Germany and, even more, Austria.

Charles's son Lawrence, after whom I am named, had rather more direct contact with the Germans during the First World War. As a major in the Honourable Artillery Company he saw action in Flanders, though by the end of the war he was in Italy. From there his battalion crossed over the Brenner Pass into the Tyrol, though it seems likely that he himself remained in Italy. After the war, he followed his father's example and became an insurance broker in the City.

While Lawrence was soldiering abroad, his son Basil was undergoing perhaps not dissimilar rigours as a boarder at a preparatory school called Rosehill, at Banstead. On at least one occasion he had reason to be thankful to the Germans. Following some misdemeanour, he was told to present himself at the study of the headmaster, Mr Browning, at eleven o'clock in the morning, to be caned. To his surprise he found the headmaster in an altogether different mood to the one he had anticipated. 'Wright minor,' said Mr Browning, in a state of some exaltation, 'I have some wonderful news for you. You are not going to be beaten. The Germans have surrendered – there is what they call an Armistice. Now go and tell the school that the Germans have surrendered!'

*

Basil's younger siblings, Barbara and her twin sister Peggy, having completed their time at school without ever being troubled by such things as public examinations or certificates, were sent to Innsbruck, where they lodged with a family called Bauer. This must have been in the late 1920s, or possibly 1930, in the year of their nineteenth birthday. At least part of the object was for my mother, a promising pianist and cellist, to continue her musical studies, though the greater purpose may have been to provide an informal

14

equivalent to a finishing school. Perhaps it was simply a question of what to do with them.

My mother always said that their mother Gladys (but always known as Paddie) had greeted the arrival of her daughters, four years on from the birth of her adored son, with something notably short of ecstasy. Certainly there was a sharp contrast between the opportunities afforded their brother Basil, who boarded at Sherborne and went on to Cambridge, and those made available to them. In later life Mummy still remembered Paddie explaining to friends on more than one occasion, and in her and Peggy's hearing, that they were 'very backward' because they were twins. The powerful devotion which Paddie lavished on her son, and which was reciprocated with an equal intensity, emphasised the relative distance she kept between herself and the twins. It cannot have helped their confidence.

Paddie was the daughter of George Marsden, who was chief designer for Wedgwood during the *art nouveau* period. An unstable personality with an early tendency towards alcoholism, he was one source for the character of Denry in Arnold Bennett's novel *The Card* (Ruth, one of Paddie's two sisters, married Bennett's brother). Of her mother, almost no report seems to have been handed down. Paddie herself was lively, intelligent, temperamental, spiteful or witty by turns, a creature of sudden passions who was equally capable of being the life and soul of the party or the death of it.

Early photographs of Barbara and Peggy show them narrowly escorted by a succession of stern, starched figures, in pairs, looking oddly like twins themselves – and identical ones at that, unlike their charges. They give the strong impression of combining effortlessly the roles of warder and governess. The twins themselves look attractive, with a mixture of openness and collusion in their expression – details which, even in these staged portraits, the camera does not miss.

*

Barbara's piano teacher in Innsbruck was Hans Zingerle, whose family was long established and even owned a castle in Gufidaun, to give the village its German name, in the Alto Adige not far from Bolzano. She evidently found this a rewarding and happy time and, presumably, a welcome respite from the difficult and dominant presence of her mother, who is said to have discouraged her from playing the piano or cello at home, particularly when it would have disturbed her afternoon rest. Yet Paddie herself had a fine mezzo-soprano voice by all accounts, and would accompany herself in popular songs, as well as Brahms and Schubert *Lieder*.

Mummy's father later gave his daughter a Broadwood boudoir grand piano made in 1911, the year of her birth: it was one of her most treasured possessions. Was the giving of it the quiet rebellion of a mild man?

*

Most families know the true history of time and chance – the sift of who and what survives, what is spoken of or glossed over; the stubborn objects outliving their owner's passion for them; the oddities of fashion; the co-editing of memory, forgetfulness and the need to forget; the photographs making it through to anonymity. And most have cumulative deposit-ories of received untruths, or at least myths which in time elide with what might have been the truth. But since lives are lived rather than researched, this process is not only natural but can give access to wider truths than genealogy, geography or chronology could ever reveal. Of course this might not apply to households where the furniture is always gleaming and the evidence arranged in neat albums: but it surely does to the majority, with their numberless ill-assorted belongings, of varying talismanic value or none, hoarded over the years. Crammed, for instance, into drawers which, despite an apparently ordered top layer, are stuffed with letters, holiday snaps, photos of unknown soldiers standing outside bell-tents, bills, addresses with no name on scraps of paper, mementos, keys to rooms and houses no longer owned, notebooks full, unused or abandoned after a few pages of handwriting, certificates of birth, marriage, divorce, death, the first locks cut from a child's hair, a beach pebble, bank statements, cheque-book stubs, broken watches, paperclips, a souvenir coffee spoon from Sorrento or Ramsgate, and throat lozenges well on the way to dissolving into syrup.

In the case of my father, Hellmut, there was little that reached us children beyond myth, and since to us he was largely a commanding absence, we had to rely on what we were told. Photographic evidence was thin, and when we were young we were never shown much of it, not even the rather fine studio portrait of his parents, Heinrich and Frieda, taken in Cologne in something like their late twenties. They seem to exude poise and serenity, but perhaps this is to read too much into the customary lack of expression of a formal pose. Heinrich bore the same first name as his father, who suffered an arm wound in the Franco-Prussian War of 1871, refused all treatment and died of an infection of the wound twenty-two years later.

Absence played a considerable part in Hellmut's life from early on. His mother died of milk fever, as puerperal sepsis was then rather delicately called, only a few days after his birth in November 1908. He then lived on his grandmother's farm in the pretty town of Melsungen, on the river Fulda near Kassel, with its tall timber-framed houses and encircling hills. Not long after, his father, an architect working for the pharmaceutical company Bayer, married again: Hellmut was eventually told by the washerwoman that Marie-Luise, the woman he had thought to be his own mother as well as the mother of his four younger siblings Wolfgang, Walter, Gertrud and Hildegard, was his stepmother. He was, in that sense, an only child. In a family photo of the time he stands against a background of dark foliage, wearing a sailor suit and clutching a model yacht. He looks winsome, even if only tentatively cheerful.

As he grew up, Hellmut developed an interest in art. He studied painting and industrial design at the Werkschule in Cologne, where he met the painter, writer and teacher Richard Seewald (in whose honour I was given my middle name), and then spent some time at the Bauhaus. The only picture of him which has survived from this time shows him in his Cologne studio. To the left, a large earthenware pot with two wavy lines round its top holds a sheaf of assorted brushes. On a rough table lie a palette and some crinkly, half-used tubes of oil paint. To the right, an easel props an unfinished painting of fishing boats drawn up on a shore.

He stands there with a self-conscious though confident expression, his hands in the pockets of a loose overall, not exactly smiling but looking as if he might risk it at some point. In his mid-twenties, he is good-looking, possibly a little vain. Strong bone structure; hair swept back from a broad forehead; clear, striking eyes with unusually long lashes; quite a long upper lip; a mouth suggestive of real stubbornness. A

18

photograph taken with the filter of a young man's dream of glory: portrait of the artist as a young Turk.

In his early twenties he also studied textile printing and worked as a freelance designer. Commissions included a mural in a newly built church, a kindergarten mural and a number of sets for the Cologne Municipal Opera. He also illustrated limited editions in German of *Huckleberry Finn* and Jack London's *The Call of the Wild*.

His career was interrupted by the increasing prominence of the Nazis. Being vehemently opposed to them, he failed to keep his mouth shut and, thanks to the equal loquacity of so-called friends, became of interest to the Blackshirts who, according to my mother, detained him for a time. His father had sufficient influence to get him released. It was decided that he should abandon his studio and even his bright blue motorbike, and leave the country.

The next episode of the story has him calling at the British Consulate in Bern to ask for a British passport, a not entirely absurd request since at the time of his birth his parents had been living in Cheshire, where his father was working on the construction of Port Sunlight. Encountering a temperature below lukewarmth, Hellmut pointed out, in the considerable German accent which he retained all his life, that he had been born in Bromborough. 'My dear chap! Then you *are* British!' the official is alleged to have declared rapturously, vaulting his desk and pumping my father's hand.

He then evidently spent some time in the South of France, where he encountered Duncan Grant, who gave him his address and said that he was to look him up if ever he found himself in London. This turned out to be no idle suggestion. When Hellmut did arrive in England, he lived for a time in accommodation in Berners Street, Soho, generously lent to him

19

by Grant. It was in nearby Maple Street, on New Year's Day 1934, that he opened the door of my uncle Basil's flat (what was he doing there? No explanation is offered by the record) to Mummy. The attraction must have been swift and mutual. Paddie disapproved of the relationship, and was strongly opposed to the idea of marriage when it surfaced, which must have helped to fan the flames. Daddy is said to have produced an ultimatum in the form of two tickets to Berwang, in Austria, where he wanted to take Mummy skiing.

A studio photograph of Barbara, taken shortly after, shows well defined, clear features. An Eton crop, long enough to show that there is a natural wave to the hair, a relaxed smile, a suggestion of humour in the eyes, all combine to convey an impression of candour and liveliness. A similar head and shoulders picture of Hellmut taken at about the same time has a greater sense of formality about it – double-breasted suit, striped shirt, dark tie with lighter dots. As in the earlier photograph taken in his Cologne studio, the most striking elements are his broad head, with already a hint of recession in the hairline; the eyes, deep-set beneath strongly delineated brows; and the quite high cheekbones. Though here he engages with the camera unsmilingly, there is a width to the mouth which somehow implies humour.

These photographs of Barbara and Hellmut work upon each other in a kind of counterpoint – her relaxed gaze, his stiffer gravitas: she being just herself, you feel; he, called to order for the occasion, out to impress more than to express.

On the 6th November 1934, the year in which they met, they were married at Marylebone Town Hall, and Miss Wright became Mrs Sail. She was just twenty-three: he was twenty days short of twenty-six. On the marriage certificate the name of the witness is given as Duncan Grant.

The colours which I most associate with Wolfy – or Siegfried Marian, to give him his proper name, are brown, pink and grey. Of these, brown is dominant, partly because that is what I first saw as he stepped in out of the snow: the mid-brown of his homburg, with its dent in the crown and a band of shiny brown silk. Then, the soft dark brown of his eyes, the different brown of his hair and moustache, the bright orange-brown stains of nicotine on his fingers. To these were added two more. Marian was a soil scientist, and he had created an assortment of organic compounds aimed at improving plant health and growth, notably a product called Actumus. I have no idea of its composition, but it took the form of a brown powder almost as fine as talc, which was despatched to customers in sacks or packets. There was also the brown of peat, in whose thera-peutic qualities he was a firm believer.

This is where pink comes in. If my sister Trinny or I (and Trinny is what I always called her, not being able to get my tongue round her full name, Catriona) had a cold or cough, we were made to sit on a high wooden stool by the gas stove, with a tea towel over our head. We had to bend forward and inhale the fumes coming from an old Chemico tin with a punctured lid, which had been filled with burning peat. Chemico, a scouring compound, was bright pink, and came in a bright pink tin. Neither Trinny nor I had much faith in this alleged remedy, in fact we hated it, but we were not offered the option of refusal.

Pink, brown and grey. Grey was a very dark grey, the grounds of charcoal which lay at the bottom of a corked medicine bottle in a liquid transparent until shaken when, like the negative of a snow globe, the grounds swirled up and briefly made the suspension opaque. This mixture was administered to us if we had an upset stomach. It had a grittiness which made swilling it feel a bit like crunching eggshell. Charcoal was also the name given to a little black kitten Marian acquired, and for which a hole was cut in the door to one of the sheds 'down under' used by Marian as a laboratory.

The office; the laboratory. Perhaps all the rooms in the house would eventually turn into such important places. Certainly Marian's business appeared to thrive. Bulky equipment was installed, a Remington typewriter about the size of a cliff face, and a Gestetner duplicator. There was a machine for heat-sealing the tough little packets in which samples of Actumus were sent by post. The first of a succession of secretaries appeared, housed in the room known as the study, where they worked alongside Mummy. Two in particular, Winifred Halliday and Doris Greenslade, became very friendly with Mummy, and almost part of the family. Winifred was a striking redhead who used impressively bright red nail varnish. Doris had dark hair which seemed to surround her pale face, with its rather worried expression, almost entirely: it reminded me of a child's drawing in which hair was scribbled all round the head. As well as book-keeping and correspondence, part of their work must have been the production and distribution of the quarterly periodical which Marian initiated. In time Winifred emigrated to the States, and Doris finally moved away.

The making of Actumus and several other products was centred on the station yard at Christow, a few miles south-west of Exeter in the Teign valley. Here various items, which may have included crushed shells, potash and lignite, were combined: it is hard to imagine that peat was not also involved. Some of the ingredients were put through a large riddle activated by an engine. The resulting compounds were finally shovelled into hundredweight sacks which were then stitched up with a large bent needle threaded with coarse twine.

A number of people were involved with the enterprise in one way or another, but were little more than names to us. These were not without resonance: among them Bill Cotter, Alistair Hornung, Mr Seward (who had a later reincarnation as a pianist at a newly opened restaurant in the city). One, Ernest Annerley, became a family friend. A love of cars may have played its part in this, since Mummy had always been fascinated by them in an entirely practical way: a broken petrol pump, dirt in the jets or a problem with the carburettor were her idea of intriguing challenges. Ernest serviced his own car – a Ford 8 at the outset, succeeded by a Hillman Minx with a gear lever on the steering column and a bench seat at the front.

A dark, sharp-faced Londoner, Ernest had a wonderful smile and a very kindly nature. He and his family lived at Cheriton Bishop, a village about fifteen miles outside Exeter. A hairdresser by training, he was always for some reason known to Trinny and me as 'Prof'. He would cut our hair in the dining-room at home, with hand clippers and the occasional use of thinning scissors which pulled horribly and made tears start to our eyes.

Sometimes I would go with Prof to Marian's railyard site, for the excitement of the drive there and back as much as anything. When I tired of watching the work, I would optimistically go and fish from a nearby bridge over the Teign: as bait I used bits of hard-boiled egg removed from the sandwiches Mummy had given me, attached to a rudimentary hook at the end of a piece of string.

An egg is responsible for keeping alive my only other memory of those who worked for Marian. At some point I went to stay (When? Why? For how long?) with Alistair Hornung and his wife near St Austell. I recall absolutely nothing about Mrs Hornung's looks, though her husband's florid complexion remains vivid, as does the solid-looking gold tooth exposed by his ready smile. But what predominates is the delectable taste of the boiled egg Mrs Hornung gave me for my supper. I ate it sitting by a large plate glass window, beyond which there was a view of a mountainous landscape dustily grey with kaolin. Nothing could have been more delicious than the tanginess of that dark yellow yolk, eaten with bread and butter.

As for Marian himself, he remains distant in memory, oddly neutral for all the drama of his first entrance and the hacking cough which, increasingly, would possess him as he sat at the dining-room table. Apart from the softness of that initial greeting, I hear no echo of his voice. And when it comes to wondering at what point he moved in, or what luggage or belongings he might have brought with him, or even how strong his Austrian accent was, the screen stays blank.

The presents which he had given us when he first arrived were supplemented at some point by two stuffed monkeys. Mine, named Bill Kick by Marian, was inflexibly set in a seated position and held a banana in one hand. Trinny's, also unmoving though in a standing posture, had green eyes and wore a red page-boy suit.

I don't remember ever seeing Marian in Mummy's bed,

though Trinny and I regularly ran into her room unannounced, in the hope of being given one of the chewy Fuller's peppermint lumps which she kept in a large tin by her bed. If there was any intimacy between them it was kept from us. Or almost: my sister has a somewhat disconcerting memory of not only seeing Marian in our mother's bed, but herself being in bed with him, playing. She has no idea what 'playing' might or might not have meant. Memory takes her no farther.

Once, as I came down from my bedroom, I heard music floating up from the hall. At the turn of the stairs I sat down, clutched the banisters and peered through. In the confined space of the hall, Marian and Mummy were dancing close together. He was holding her lightly round the waist, and she had a hand on his shoulder. They held their other hand joined. Somehow they managed to avoid bumping into the walls, though they did sometimes brush against the coats hanging on their hooks. At one point they twirled out of sight down the short passage leading to the front door, but soon returned as they had to if they were to keep moving. The music, coming from the gramophone in the drawing-room, was loud and quite slow. It held them in its spell. They were gazing intently at one another, and my mother was smiling dreamily. They were oblivious to me. Something felt all wrong: it was as if I had eavesdropped on a plot. The melody seemed to gloat; the secretive huskiness of the instruments excluded me.

Suddenly I had to escape back up the stairs. I went as quickly and quietly as I could, rushed into my room and lay on the bed. My breathing sounded unnaturally fast and loud. It was not enough to shut out the sound of the smooth complicities wafting up the stairwell.

25

In the spring following the move to Exeter, when the weather had finally relented, Trinny and I started to attend Edgerton Park School, the establishment just a few minutes' walk away at the intersection of Union Road and Pennsylvania Road. Although a girls' school, it tolerated boys up to the age of seven. My scant memories of it include making cardboard models (*fold sheet B along the perforated line, tuck flange A into flap D, glue onto base at C*), maypole dancing, watching giant girls with coloured sashes playing netball, and the traditional striking of bargains over the showing of girls' knickers. There was also a deal of hymn singing: it must have been here that I first encountered Mrs Alexander's far-away green hill, the one apparently robbed of a city wall, which was to cause me such trouble.

A school photograph taken in the summer of 1947 shows Trinny and me sitting cross-legged at the front, the location reserved for new arrivals. I look cuboid and dishevelled, with tie knotted slackly and hair unparted; Trinny is more tidily turned out. Rather like Daddy in the picture of him holding the sailing boat, we seem uncertain whether to smile or frown. In the middle section of the middle row, the all-female staff presents a formidable display of rage in reserve and sensible shoes. Beneath the photograph, the school motto, *Sursum Corda*, challenges us to lofty aspiration.

At some point in the year Elisabeth from Austria arrived, the first of three au pair girls and in many ways the least colourful. Perhaps it was just that we were taken up with our own lives, on which she seemed to make little impact, though she must have given us much practical help. Or perhaps those pleasant, quite serious features indicated an unassuming mildness which we ought to have appreciated more.

As with Marian, we knew only that Elisabeth came from Austria, with no further details of background or location. She occupied the narrow bedroom next to mine on the top floor. With its iron bedstead and small bamboo dressing-table, it was a cramped, rather gloomy space. One small window looked out on a tall tree which blocked the light and, when there was a high wind, tapped scratchily at the pane.

*

Like all small children, we lived not so much in a linear flow of time, but from one intense episode to the next, creatures of appetite and curiosity, finding our freedom in the ample gaps between adult routines and demands. We began to explore the territory. There were danger points, some more threatening than others. The most obvious was the dusty, cobwebbed yew tree in the front garden of a house we passed on the way to school. Here Edgar Lorch, a dark-haired boy older than us, would conceal himself and leap out, sneering and bent on aggression. Down the hill, close to the football ground, was where Membury the newsagent lived: a tiny man, shorter than Alexander Pope, who wore black gaiters and an inky black waistcoat over a striped shirt with no collar. He was almost as yellow as the old copies of *Hotspur*, *Dandy* and *Radio Fun* in his front window, and his house smelt of cat piss. He peered out from small black-framed glasses. Once, sent by Mummy to pay him, we went into his back room, which seemed a very risky thing to do, and saw him bring out a black cashbox which he opened furtively.

27

Nearby was the railway bridge where we would stand waiting for a train to pass beneath and send up great gouts of white steam and particles of soot. Then the bridge itself quaked beneath our feet.

Notwithstanding Elisabeth and her successors, we were left very much to ourselves, sufficiently so for us to be known locally, rather absurdly, as 'the orphans of the street'. We never really got to know the neighbours or, come to that, anyone else in the road. On one side there was Mr Morgan, whom we were warned not to annoy, so that we became very wary on the rare occasions that we caught sight of him in his garden, which ran down beside ours, separated from it only by wires running between concrete posts. His garden seemed wild, but it may just have been that he had decided to keep a firewall of couch grass and tall nettles between him and us. Such was the combined effect of Mummy's warning and his scowling presence that even when he was not in sight we thought twice about retrieving a ball if it had strayed onto his land.

On the other side lived Mrs Smith and her family: if there was a Mr Smith in residence, we never saw him. The Smith children would sometimes stare down at us from their conservatory, which was at a higher level than ours, at one end of a verandah. We must have gone into their house now and then, because I remember one occasion on which Mrs Smith impressed us hugely by throwing an amount of polish onto a struggling open fire, where it crackled and flared as if it had been a firework.

Also encountered in the garden, and as daunting as Mr Morgan but a great deal closer, was our gardener, Mr Dart. We never knew his first name, and communication was difficult because he was deaf. This not only made us inaudible to him, but his own speech was blurred and abrupt. He was swarthy, with a shock of black hair. He always seemed very bad-tempered, but this may have been in part an effect of his deafness. He arrived on an old bicycle, invariably wearing a collarless striped shirt, just like Mr Membury, and old blue pin-striped trousers clamped to his legs with bicycle clips. Trinny and I were frightened of him.

The other frequenter of the garden was Mr Graham, an altogether more benign presence. He wore a straw hat, and had gold-rimmed glasses behind which he blinked frequently. He seemed to us like an extremely old but affable lizard. He grew vegetables on a strip of land running alongside the main strip, from which it was separated only by a narrow path. The land belonged to us, but would have been too much for Mr Dart. Mr Graham's part of the garden was impressively well ordered, with taut lines of string, and seedlings which always seemed to sprout eagerly and in disciplined ranks.

Otherwise, we really saw few people, adults or children. This relative isolation may have had as much to do with the nature of Trinny's and my relationship with one another, as with Mummy's circumstances and the kind of place Exeter was. We would spend much of our time happily in the kingdom of the garden. Mummy had bought a secondhand Wendy house for us. Made of plywood and painted grey, with two latticework windows, one on either side of the door, it was very simple and could be dismantled easily: the four walls just hooked onto each other at the corners. When we weren't playing with that, we would be busy digging a long, grave-shaped hole nearby. Once it was deep enough, we would roof it with a sheet of rusting corrugated iron, then crawl into it and lie there, listening to our own breathing

29

and trying to keep alight a stub of candle for which we had scooped out a niche.

*

It was said that the ground on which the city stood had once been a volcano, and that the local red sandstone owed its colour to the impact of the flames which had once roared sky-ward with a cargo of rocks and hot cinders. At some distant moment, between its quiet non-existence at the bottom of deep waters and the final cooling of the magma, this had been the site of dramatic, violent events.

It was impossible now to imagine such cataclysmic forces at work: not only the ground but the lives lived on it seemed to have solidified permanently. Even the damage inflicted by one of Hitler's Baedeker raids, terrible as it was, had failed to alter fundamentally the city's presiding spirit of steadfast-ness: not for nothing was its motto *Semper Fidelis*. But a corol-lary of this was a suspicion of outsiders and an intensely provincial intolerance of any perceived impropriety: and after all, for many Devonians foreigners were people who came from anywhere outside the county.

On any scale of local unacceptability Mummy would have managed a staggeringly high score. As a divorcée, she was axiomatically to be despised or, at best, pitied. To then take a lover put her well beyond the pale. And a German at that! (Well, Austrian then, but where was the difference?) And as if all that were not enough, to then import foreign girls (Austrian, too, would you believe!) to put upon those poor children with their foreign ways, while Mrs S. herself cavorted with her man! Terrible, to see the poor mites wandering along hand in hand, as lost as the babes in the wood ...

Hand in hand. Isolated by our closeness to one another, and by no means miserable. As twins, not one but biparous, oddly apart but together. Womb neighbours: blood neighbours. Had we lain there side by side, as we sucked in life and swelled moment by moment, or had we been folded into one another like the figure 69, 'fully interlocking' as jigsaws described themselves? Like that we would have formed a circle, protected, a small round planet afloat in the dark, the two of us held as if in a transparent envelope, maybe ourselves aglow as some fish-eggs are, our two umbilical cords waving eerily like weed in the flow. Held in suspension, perfectly attuned to each other's burgeoning existence: facsimile of a wordless peaceable kingdom. After this, how could anything be adequate? Beyond the confines of the maternal wholeness, there could surely be only fragments: words, jagged comparisons, measures of ground gained or lost. No hand-dug tunnel in the garden could match the womb.

We devised a secret language, a matter of prefixing each word with 'tw' – a nod towards our being twins, and simple enough. Spoken at speed, it could be still intelligible to us and baffling to others. But it was hard to pronounce at any pace – twif twyou twee twhat twI twean. Later, there came more elaborate codes transposing the usual alphabetical order, with the keys written down in notebooks. In the den we had made under the basement stairs we hammered the coded words into the crumbling plaster of the wall, using carpet tacks to delineate the letters.

*

A powerful regular feature of our lives was the kids' morning on Saturdays at the Odeon, a great beached whale of a building only about fifteen minutes' walk away. Here we joined an army of precocious wolf-whistlers for a programme of cartoons, newsreels, drama and comedy – a first taste of Chaplin, Harold Lloyd, and Laurel and Hardy. Roy Rogers featured, and there was also a serial which carried over from week to week. A particularly gruesome one was a drama about the Ku Klux Klan, which culminated in the hero being burned alive at the stake, himself hooded like a Klansman, the villains having neatly arranged a convenient case of mistaken identity. The victim was seen to have his hands and feet bound, as the flames licked round him. As he writhed and twisted, the hood over his head, with its mere slits and tall white point, became more horribly expressive of pain than his actual features might have been.

Much less horrifying was the Pathé News, with its cheerful blinking cockerel perched in a garland of leaves and roses. In the world of Pathé, disaster was rarely other than thrilling, accompanied as it invariably was by Dick Bartonesque music, and with the triumphalist tones of the voice-over guaranteeing that everything would turn out well, more often than not thanks to a British achievement of one kind or another.

The cartoons showed the world at its least vulnerable: the characters were india-rubber and could pick themselves up after any battering. Here comes Tom, careering at speed round the furniture in pursuit of Jerry, then down the hallway, out of the house, a skidding turn round the broomstick in the yard, along the street dodging the traffic, turning sharp left then right, generating small puffs of cloud at his heels, then along more streets, sending a dustbin lid bowling away on its edge, then down the lane to the high cliff where Jerry miraculously brakes and shimmies sideways, leaving Tom to run on over the edge. He stays there gulping and blinking, running on air, with paws flailing, till the illusion can no longer support him and he plummets like a stone down the lift shaft of gravity. Splat! And overhead the little mouse peers cheekily from the clifftop, giggling delightedly.

In the interval, when the huge silky curtains, backlit in orange, were drawn across, the usherettes sashayed down the aisles, trays with beakers of dilute orange squash and tubs of ice cream slung round their neck. Then, sleepwalking through the sweet-sour atmosphere of confectionery and disinfectant, a blind man was led to a piano at the front corner of the stage. It was his task to accompany the children in such songs as 'Tipperary', 'Pack up your troubles' and 'My bonny lies over the ocean', the words projected onto a small screen lowered in front of the curtains. We sang raucously, without feeling, let alone any notion of the songs' origins.

*

Almost as frightening as the Ku Klux Klan film was one of the final floats in the University College's Rag Week parade, which Trinny and I went into town to see. Most of the procession had gone by, its tableaux borne along on the backs of lorries – a jungle scene with two students in ape suits; Elizabeth I on a slightly wobbly throne; doctors in bloodstained coats, one wielding a hacksaw, another pulling strings of pale sausages from the innards of a supine patient. Next, it was a float draped with Robin Hood and his Merrie Men: a small forest of stocky thighs in green tights with, to one side, Maid Marian blushing beneath her wimple and Friar Tuck beaming cloddishly from under an obvious tonsure wig. Then came a lorry draped in black. It drew abreast of us and was forced to a halt by the slowness of the floats up ahead. It was stark enough. There was a block of wood on the floor and, beside it, a large man dressed in a black jerkin and black trousers. His bare arms were folded and resting on a gleaming axe; a smear of red ran along the edge of its blade. It was somehow all the more disturbing that there was no victim to be seen. The man stood motionless, facing us. He had a small black eye-mask: behind it, his eyes glittered ferociously. His mouth was grimly set.

Why did masks always frighten us so? Or perhaps it was something to do with that smear of blood.

*

It was hard to tell where the hymn ended and the nightmare began. 'There is a green hill far away …' Green. 'Saved by his precious Blood.' Red. The red blood of Christ falling, drop after drop, onto the green grass. 'He hung and suffered there.' Like the man in the film, his hooded head hanging forward as the smoke and fire reached into him. The hooded figure of Christ on the cross. 'We cannot tell what pain he had to bear.' The pain of the nails. The pain of the flames. And then, 'his redeeming Blood', with a capital B in the hymn book – the Blood you had to trust, the Blood to wash you white, to rinse away your shame and guilt into the green grass. The iron taste of it as it washed over your lips and bubbled into your mouth. The taste that lay in your mouth when at last you woke up.

Somehow all this became incorporated into a dream which also involved a chase: not a harmless Tom and Jerry one, but a flight from malign forces. It always ended in the same ineluctable way. I would reach a place of supposed safety (often, grassy ruins) and, exhausted, sink down to rest. It was then that the demons, or whatever they were, closed in. Try as I might, there was no escape: to run was to find oneself on a treadmill. I screamed, and would wake with a start to find myself on the landing outside my room, actually screaming and shaking the banisters at the top of the stairs with both hands.

To begin with, Mummy would run upstairs to comfort me. But the dream became its own treadmill, happening again and again. It was decided that the best way to break this cycle would be a change of scene. I was sent to a children's home somewhere in or near to Bradninch, to the east of Exeter. I cannot recall exactly when this occurred, or for how long I stayed there, or much about the other children there, but I think that I was five. I do remember very clearly getting off a bus in the country with Mummy, and walking down a long tree-lined drive which dipped, then rose, between iron railings at the edge of fields.

In the entrance hall to the place stood a magnificent rocking-horse which I was invited to ride while Mummy went with the matron to her office. The horse was dappled, and had a real leather saddle and shiny stirrups. When Mummy emerged, she said goodbye quite quickly, while the matron encouraged me to have another ride. By the time I dismounted, Mummy was nowhere to be seen.

Then there was the matter of the milk, a drink I detested however it was served, and at whatever temperature. It made me gag. There was no allowance for such distastes in the home's régime. This resulted in a great deal of time spent in the dining-room, with its sour odours of curd and rotting dishcloths, long after meals had ended and the other children had been liberated to play outside. Matron sat at the head of the table, and I some way down, with the ghastly bluish pillar of milk in a glass in front of me. 'Drink your milk,' she would repeat at intervals, in a voice made all the more threatening by its controlled softness. In the end, but only after more than token resistance, I did. 'There now. Wasn't that silly?' What was really silly was my slowness to realise that she didn't want to be there any more than I did. Once this dawned on me, I put it to the test by deliberately knocking over the glassful of milk. It spread widely, in the way that spilt liquid always does, and dripped from the table edge onto the bench. Equally rewarding was the displacement of the soft voice in favour of trembling anger. I was made to clear up the mess and say sorry. But the glass was not refilled and I was not kept in again.

Once I returned home, the recurrent nightmare seemed to have stopped, or at any rate to have been driven into a corner, a threat suppressed if not solved.

*

Whether or not it was a device to ward off future nightmares I don't know, but Mummy bought two little angels, one each, to fix to the headboard of our beds. They were in a sitting position, with their knees bent, so that they could perch on ledges. They were more like *putti* than angels: stubby wings sprouted from their shoulders. *Putti* makes them sound too ornate: they were moulded in pale green plastic, and their only virtue was that they glowed eerily when the light was put out.

Beyond these tutelary watchers, Mummy's attitude to religion seemed vague. She liked the idea of shepherds washing their socks by night, and the logic of her own childhood error in thinking that her uncle was God: *Harold be Thy name*. We had been christened in our first year in the little church of St Mary's at Cheriton Bishop, where Prof lived, but thereafter there had not been much, if any, churchgoing. When Trinny and I began walking into town on Sundays to attend the service at St Stephen's, a small church in the High Street,

Mummy neither encouraged nor discouraged us, but didn't think to come too. Guardian angels did, though, appeal to her as an idea, and she also suggested vaguely on a number of occasions that we ought to kneel by our beds and say our prayers before going to sleep. The temperature in our rooms was not always conducive to this, and we had no concept of self-improvement by hardship. It seemed more important to lie low and thaw your feet out on the hot water bottle Mummy had provided. She had made a cover, to moderate its initial stinging heat.

The nomadism of my parents' early married life may have been exaggerated by the fragmentary nature of what I know about it, but it still seems considerable: witness the number of stamps in Barbara's passport of the period. Within three months of their marriage they went to France, Austria and Germany, the latter despite Hellmut's hasty departure a year earlier. In the summer they went to France and Spain, and in November to Cologne for a month, presumably to see Hellmut's family. They returned to England just after Christmas. Visits to banks abroad in this and subsequent years to cash travellers' cheques, all recorded in Barbara's passport, suggest that they were being given financial support by her parents.

The following year, 1936, saw them skiing in Berwang in the spring, then spending almost the whole of July in Spain, at Tossa de Mar on the Costa Brava. It must have been on this visit that they bought a tiny house just out of the town. It lay in an empty valley beyond the cemetery, at the end of a dusty, unsurfaced track. The house would have been very cheap, lacking all amenities as it did. There was no electricity, and water was drawn up from a small well in a bucket. The well was also where watermelons were let down to cool: catching them in the bucket was a knack. Cooking was done on a stove fuelled by charcoal, and ice had to be got in large slabs from the ice factory on the other side of town and brought home wrapped in a blanket.

Tossa itself was idyllic – a small bay embracing shining

blue waters, with the towers and walls of its old castle on a headland, and few tourists. The political situation must also have deterred all but the boldest visitors, let alone prospective house buyers. It was in mid-July that General Mola, soon joined by Franco, rose up against the Republican government.

By the end of the month they had left again, electing to drive rather than take advantage of the British destroyer deployed to bring British citizens away from the developing civil war. They had to stop often on the way – one village after another was barricaded – and produce the travel permit issued to them by the Revolutionary Committee in Tossa. Barbara never forgot having a pistol held waveringly a few inches from her head by a youth examining their papers.

They went first to Cologne then to Ronco, in Switzerland on the north-west shore of Lake Maggiore, where Richard Seewald had settled after prudently migrating from Germany; then to friends in Basle, before going on to the south of France in September and back to Cologne, where they again remained till after Christmas.

The diaries kept by Barbara ought to be a good source of information about their travels, but with one exception they are logbooks more than journals, largely confined to a record of the troubles afflicting their blue Ford 8 and to the minutiae of meals and hotels. The reader discovers a great deal about the details of their journeying – where petrol was taken on, the cost of it and the car's mileage at that point, when and where oil was changed, a puncture mended, the jets cleaned, a broken fuel line repaired; or how, stuck in deep snow near the top of the Gotthard Pass, they were towed out by some Swiss soldiers who, luckily, happened along in a jeep. In addition to such episodes, diligent notes are kept of a delicious goulasch here, a poor hotel there, a *Wiener Schnitzel* eaten with relish on the way from A to B, the ingredients of a picnic en route. There is the occasional flurry of detail: the money Barbara lost in Venice as a novice gambler; going to see Magritte in Brussels and being given one of his pictures (apparently later destroyed in a Baker Street depository during the blitz); Barbara going for treatment for sciatica to the thermal baths in Abano, where the sweat poured off her as she lay packed in hot mud. Twenty minutes like that each morning before five minutes in a mineral bath, followed by breakfast and a rest.

There are also passing references to friends and encounters with strangers, but not much about museums or concerts, though they went to both. It seems that the real centre of their interest, apart from Hellmut's painting, was the business of travel itself. In three years they covered over 25,000 miles in their plucky little Ford: not much by today's standards, but a considerable mileage then. The important thing was to keep on the move and not ask too many questions about purpose and destination. It was a kind of pan-European bumming, with not much money but plenty of variety and company, as well as an odd sense of community: you were quite likely to meet in, say, Geneva the couple you saw some months before in Dubrovnik.

Now and then the diaries admit to doubts about where to go next and what to do. But 1937 seems to have been different, and luckily this is the one period for which Barbara kept a journal rather than a log, beginning it in England in March 1937 while Hellmut was scouting for a cheap place to live and work in Basle. The journal begins on a note of considerable self-deprecation, with my mother describing

herself as weak-minded and in some way deficient in character. She expresses her gratitude to Hellmut for teaching her so
much. There is something both sad and innocent about this.
The journal goes on to give a good idea of her interest in art
and artists, books (large chunks of Ford Madox Ford are
copied out) and, above all, music. Motors and meals are put
in perspective.

In mid-May, having failed to find quarters in Basle, they set
off for Yugoslavia. After an exhilarating journey, but also a
tiring one given the state of the Yugoslav roads, they found
themselves still a hundred miles short of their proposed destination, Dubrovnik, and were further discouraged by being
told that the town was full. They thought they would go on to
Sarajevo. On the way they stopped at Makarska for a beer,
and liked the place so much that they decided to stay. At the
Hotel Meteor, on the sea front, they were able to take a room
very cheaply, with an adjacent one for Hellmut to use as a studio for no extra charge.

The two and a half months that they spent in Makarska,
from mid-May 1937 to the end of July, must have been among
the happiest of their travelling years, even though they could
hardly ignore the deteriorating international situation, as
noted by Barbara in her journal. But for the moment they
seemed to have found a magical place where Hellmut could
work and together they could look out over the harbour and
the sea. One day a seaplane landed, and on another an entire
circus, the Circus Olympio, disembarked from an incoming
sailing ship. Once a Yugoslav submarine surfaced and came
into the port, followed shortly by a French one. Both moored
at the quay and invited tours of inspection. On another occasion the *King Alexander*, a coastal steamer of some size, made
its way into harbour after nightfall, blazing with lights. In

41

many ways Makarska must have had something of the same appeal as Tossa: boats, the sea, cheap living.

They got to know a local couple, Mr and Mrs Klarić, and were taken to local festivals and dances. There was a trip on a steamer to Dubrovnik, and visits to Split and Mostar. In mid-June there was torrential rain and, towards the end of July, at eight in the morning, enough of an earth tremor to set everything in the room quivering. On the evening of the same day fireworks and flares were let off round the harbour to celebrate the birthday of the Croatian party leader.

Above all, there was Hellmut's work, landscapes and still lifes, with no less than fifteen oil paintings completed during the stay at Makarska, according to my mother, as well as gouaches, watercolours and pastels. This seems an astonishing tally.

I still have an oil painting of the island of Korčula, off the Adriatic coast halfway between Split and Dubrovnik, given to me on one of my father's rare visits to Exeter. In the foreground are two clinker-built rowing boats, one completely out of the water, the other lying on its side in a small stone enclosure attached to the quay. Across a strait of rich aquamarine water lies the island, flat as a biscuit, crammed with houses, churches and other buildings enclosing streets hidden from view. In the background, a vaguely defined range of mountains on the mainland, pale as clouds. If I had to choose a single picture of my father's to keep, this might well be the one. This has something to do with the fact that it has always hung close by my bed ever since it was given to me, but more with the emblematic values with which I came to endow it. I love the suggestion of the island closed in on itself, hermetic, played off against the possibility of reaching it implied by the boats: the dimension of secrecy and the tantalising width of the strait combining with the supposition of a quest. If there is a secret, it is an open one. Then there is the notion of a domain which, though impenetrable, presents a pleasing exterior to the world, in the form of the island's overall shapeliness: and, inseparable in my mind from secrecy, the possibility of shelter and safety.

At the same time that Daddy gave me the picture of Korčula, he gave Trinny a picture too, one which I have always thought rather disappointing by comparison. Also an oil, it shows the corner of a house with a wall at the top of a hill. There is a bench against the wall, and a road leading down. In the background is a cotton-wool wisp of a distant island, with a tiny dark boat moored at its edge. I wonder now whether this might have been a view looking out from Korčula, though as the island appears in my picture it looks much too flat to accommodate any gradient. According to Mummy, Daddy never worked *in situ*, and it may be that this picture, like many, was a composite of places he had seen.

Other pictures, not necessarily those painted in Yugoslavia, bear distinctly Makarskan traces. There are two gouaches, for instance, which show glimpses of a harbour and boats, seen from the interior of a room with tall, partly closed shutters: shutters very like those shown all along the front of the building in the deckled postcard I have of the Hotel Meteor as it then was. These pictures, too, intriguingly balance shadow and light, what is seen and what may be only hinted at.

Despite the relatively settled nature of the time spent in Makarska, a note of unease comes through in my mother's journal. This seems to be compounded of Hellmut's restlessness, his tendency to go out on his own, often returning with new friends and sometimes with a throbbing head, and continuing uncertainty about the future, both personal and political. By now they had arranged for their belongings in England to be sent to Tossa, so they clearly intended to live there. It cannot have helped that these chattels went missing for a time on the way. And the very success of their stay in Makarska might have increased the desire to find a home, particularly on my mother's part. Perhaps, too, she was thinking of the possibility of children, though if so she never confided this to her journal.

For the moment, it was to be more travelling, with a card from Hans Zingerle urging them to come to Summersberg, the family castle in Gufidaun. There was also the impact of someone telling them that Makarska would be impossibly crowded later in the summer, with up to three thousand visitors. They would not have liked to think of their enclave of enchantment overrun.

Off they went on another obstacle race, involving the carburettor and petrol pump yet again, a cylinder head gasket, a lost screw, a membrane which would require a replacement to be sent out from London, and any number of punctures. Here the journal reverts to a logbook, before it opens out again to describe the month and a half spent largely at Summersberg, with the occasional foray north to Innsbruck.

In fact it makes rather odd reading, not unlike a convoluted opera synopsis. What it seems to describe is a series of manoeuvres – Barbara, Hellmut and Hans performing a kind of edgy dance, if not actually jockeying for position. Barbara plays the piano a lot; Hans plays to her. Hellmut decides to take up the piano. Barbara and Hans go walking. The three of them go for a walk with Hans's mother. They all go to Innsbruck, where Hans shows them round and plays them

Debussy, Stravinsky and Satie at his flat in the Lieberstrasse. They return to Gufidaun. Hellmut goes to Florence for a few days, writing from there to say that he is having more trouble with the petrol pump and that, the city being impossibly hot, he is going on to Assisi: during this time Hans and Barbara celebrate Hans's birthday together. At his brother Berthold's suggestion Hans plays 'Clair de Lune' to Barbara: the moon is obligingly full. Hans buys piano music for Hellmut. Barbara falls into a depression. Hellmut returns; Hans gives him his first piano lesson. The car develops a problem with the gearbox and Hellmut has to take it into Bolzano for repair. For Barbara's birthday Hans gives her the piano works of Philip Emmanuel Bach. Hans goes back to Innsbruck, while Barbara and Hellmut wait for the arrival of spare parts for the car from England. Finally, having decided to go to Brussels for the winter, they are able to head north, lingering for a few days in Innsbruck to spend more time with Hans.

Once in Brussels, it took them only forty-eight hours to find an unfurnished flat, later relinquished in favour of a studio which was cheaper and warmer. They were able to resume a more settled existence, to Barbara's delight. Peggy came over for a weekend, with their father visiting in December. But a plan for Barbara to visit Innsbruck in February had to be scrapped for lack of money, and in April 1938 they returned to England, having been abroad for eleven months. On arrival they traded in the Ford 8 for a second-hand Ford V8 Pilot.

The pace of their travels slackened, despite a trip in the summer which took them to Ronco, Gufidaun and finally back to Brussels, where they decided to give up the studio. By January the next year they were living at Highpoint,

Lubetkin's north London landmark. But they had unfinished business in Tossa and, with the Spanish Civil War over in the spring of 1939, they decided to go out to the house there. In the summer they set off, going via Ronco to visit Richard Seewald, as they had the year before. Given the increasingly dire political news, they decided to pause. Sitting in a café in Ascona they heard Britain's declaration of war on Germany. Back at Ronco, they picked up a broadcast by the British ambassador in Geneva. The last train for British passport holders would be leaving on the afternoon of the following Sunday, 10th September 1939. Cars would have to be left behind. A maximum of three suitcases would be allowed. So their wandering ended on a packed train moving slowly through the dark towards the Channel ports, and an even more crowded boat. LAST REFUGEE TRAIN OUT OF EUROPE, ran a headline in the *Daily Telegraph*.

This must have been a difficult time for Hellmut, with his many German relatives. He became a conscientious objector and, early in 1940, joined the Auxiliary Fire Service. Shortly afterwards he took on a job as a driver for the W. V. S. He had acquired a printing press, and someone at Highpoint informed the police, presumably with the implication that he might be turning out enemy propaganda. He was visited by a Military Policeman described by Barbara as 'polite and apologetic'.

Then Barbara became pregnant. She knitted a set of baby clothes, and embroidered an anchor on the baby's night-gowns and pillowcases, using as a pattern the anchor which Hellmut had designed and adopted as his emblem. It had a large ring at the top of the shank, with one end of the stock turned up, the other down, giving the impression of a figure dancing. Close to the anchor was a single star.

46

In November the baby, a girl, blonde and blue-eyed, strangled herself with the umbilical cord at birth. When H.M.S. *Hood* was sunk by the *Bismarck* the following May, Mummy asked that the baby clothes with their dancing anchor be given to the widow of one of the sailors.

After Elisabeth returned to Austria, her place was taken by Eva Meissner, the daughter of a far from well-to-do Viennese family. Lively and forthright, she had a warmth of personality which quickly endeared her to Mummy and, even more, to Trinny and me. She had dark hair, brown eyes, skin which tanned easily, the faint beginnings of a moustache and a great sense of fun. Her English improved rapidly and there was something loveable in the way that she held the words at arm's length even as she pronounced them, as if acknowledging that they were inherently rather strange, or almost beyond her. She was also very well organised, as suggested by her wonderfully neat handwriting. She always used purple ink and, when she wrote letters, the paper and envelopes she used were fine as tissue paper.

Occasionally, if we were being too cheeky, she would threaten to smack our mouths with a wooden spoon, but we knew that she was quite incapable of this. On the contrary, she was our great ally, and the three of us almost constituted a household of our own. Much time was spent in the basement, at one occupation or another. We would help Eva to turn the handle of the great mangle or to feed sheets into it, then watch the ghost-sheet of milky water cascade into the zinc tub below.

Eva was also an excellent cook, unlike Mummy, who hated cooking, and we were soon enjoying as many Austrian dishes as post-war rationing and shortages would allow her to conjure. Her puddings and cakes were particularly memorable, from *Zwetschgenknödel*, tart little damsons encased in small dumplings and sprinkled with sugar, to a cake which, combining yellow and brown in a mysterious way, looked like a giant doughnut, with a hole in the middle. Soups were good, too, and goulasch, and cabbage salad with caraway seeds, and *Rouladen*, beef tied into little parcels with black cotton, and – almost anything that she put on the table.

It was Eva, too, who introduced us to *Manners Neapolitaner*, little rectangular wafers filled with layers of a hazelnut chocolate paste. They came in foil, with a pink paper wrapper which had a line drawing in blue of the *Stefanskirche*, the cathedral of Vienna, with its tall thin spire and steeply pitched zig-zag roof. Mummy, who had a very sweet tooth, loved them as much as we did, and soon persuaded a shop in Exeter to import them. Twenty or so packets were packed in a pink carton the shape and size of a shoebox, again deco-rated with the *Stefanskirche*. No dentist would have approved of them, but then Mummy, whose own teeth were removed wholesale about this time, had no sense of what was dentally good or bad. A few years later, when sweets finally came off the ration, she would leave a small bar of chocolate by our beds from time to time, last thing at night; and she trusted us to clean our teeth rather than insisting on it.

The Manner factory, Eva told us, was not far from her home in Vienna, and she recalled that when the wind was in the right direction you got the sweet smell of chocolate, modified just a little by hazelnut.

Mummy's main interest, in the kitchen, was the prepara-tion of breakfast coffee, which she always carried out by what she termed 'the Viennese method'. This involved placing a quantity of freshly ground coffee in a large saucepan, heating it over the gas for a few seconds, then adding hot water and bringing it to the boil, until steam began to pout through the crust of grounds accumulated on the surface. The crucial thing then was to stir in a tablespoonful of cold water, to persuade the grounds to settle. It was all done with the reverence of the true coffee addict: as much ritual as recipe.

Mummy also revered wine, though she always drank in moderation and very easily became tipsy. Nuits St Georges and Châteauneuf du Pape seemed to command her particular respect, though it may well have been saying the words which she enjoyed, as much as downing the stuff. (Daddy, on the other hand, as I discovered later, simply referred to wine as 'booze', managing to invest the word with a soft attractiveness, and downed it considerably.) Occasionally she had a Dubonnet, its herbal sweetness offset by a small piece of lemon.

In the sheds 'down under', Trinny and I found an empty beer bottle with a nubbled stopper which, licked, tasted bitter. The bottle had a label with a black horse, which made me associate it with the pub along the road, the Victoria Arms – a mysterious place, with its frosted glass doors that swung to and fro, sending a yeasty smell out into the street and allowing a fleeting glimpse of the dark interior. Here too, on the sign above the green tilework of the pub's exterior, was a black horse.

*

The Austrian tendency was not limited to food and drink. Over the years Marian and Mummy built up a remarkable collection of Viennese and Austrian songs, many of them sung by Erich Kunz, others by Hermann Leopoldi and most far more sugary than any of Eva's desserts. Larmoyant violins, attenuated accordion notes, or plangent tones from the zither accompanied professions of longing and love tinged with folksy philosophising: 'Luck's a bird', 'My mother was a Viennese girl', 'The Danube flows so blue', 'If the Lord God's not willing'. Drink was represented by a pæan to the Austrian wine Gumpoldskirchner ('Ah, if only it rained nothing but pure Gumpoldskirchner'). Many of these songs were rendered in the broadest Viennese, a virtual argot which elides sentiment and schmaltz all too easily. In a slightly different vein were the records of folk dances, their syncopations accompanied by drumming shoes and slapped *Lederhosen*; and yodelling songs with their strangulated jollity. The onion domes, chalets and flowery meadows on the record sleeves seemed a fairyland only just compatible with so much noise and leaping.

No shortage of German names, either, among the composers and titles of the classical records stacked next to the gramophone. Ah, the gramophone: that household god probably took up more of my childhood hours than anything else. Housed in a shiny black cabinet about the size of a sideboard, it had a cream-coloured woven rectangle in front, from which the sound issued. It included a wireless with a glowing dark orange display of the stations to which you could tune it, their names as exotic to us as anything in the *Arabian Nights* – Hilversum, Luxembourg, Daventry, Athlone, Budapest. We would sit by it with Mummy and listen to Wilfred Pickles, or Ted Ray, or 'Life with the Lyons', while she darned socks under a close lamp, using her wooden mushroom with a spring like a bicycle clip round its rim to hold them in place. This, along with an amazing array of needles in pleasing tiny packets, brightly coloured reels of cotton and silk, wool wound round cards, hooks and eyes, buttons, thimbles, bias

51

binding and rufflette, was kept in a rectangular workbox of dark stained oak. (The cotton reels, like gramophone records, had holes in the middle. Once the cotton was used up, the reels could be made into vehicles propelled by a rubber band, with the help of a candle stub and two matchsticks: with notches scored along their edges, they could surmount minor obstacles in a manner reminiscent of a beetle.)

I loved the actual machinery of the gramophone. The turntable had a U-shaped prong with two raised nipples placed horizontally to one side of it: this made it possible to put up to six or so records above the one you were playing, one on top of the other, with the edge of the bottom one balanced on the prong, and the hole at the centre of the record caught on the notch in the steel spindle rising at the centre of the turntable. At the conclusion of each record, the arm with the needle would jerk clear, and the prong nod forward so that the next record was dislodged, falling onto the turntable but sufficiently cushioned by air not to break. The arm would then swing back, lowering itself to the first grooves of the newly arrived record. In this way it was possible, even with 78s, to listen to, say, a complete Brandenburg concerto without budging from your seat. It never ceased to amaze me that this arrangement could possibly work.

The records themselves, large as dinner plates, had all the attraction of rare stamps. Their labels were things of beauty: the purple-blue of Columbia, the red or, sometimes, black of His Master's Voice, with the white dog bending its cocked ear to the blaring cone of the loudspeaker. There were even some old one-sided records, thicker than the others with, etched on the blank side, an instruction not to try playing it that way up. Among the performers were Amelita Galli-Curci, Vladimir de Pachmann complete with a guttural, breathy introduction to a Chopin waltz which he then played – and Ernest Lush, living up to his name with a sentimental rendering of 'Oh, for the wings of a dove'.

Sentimentality was not just Mr Lush's prerogative. As I grew up I felt increasingly sorry for Schubert. Listening to his Unfinished Symphony, it made me sad to think of the frail, bespectacled figure depicted in a book of my mother's, and his dying so young: falling to the ground in the middle of composing, his feet flying up, as I envisaged it, with a dripping quill in his hand and the symphony never to be completed.

There were plenty of Austrian and German names, too, in the stack of piano music kept under the piano in the drawing-room. Even the musical box in the basement, a miraculous thing about the size of a child's coffin, though heavier, its lid decorated inside with a chorus line of nymphs wrapped only in gauzy but strategically located veils, included the Austrian national anthem in its repertoire.

Most of all, when it came to music, there was the Broad-wood boudoir grand piano, largest and most precious of our possessions. Its sturdiness was emphasised by the effect of foreshortening that it shared with all baby grands – as if it had been in a collision and survived intact but compressed a little. There was almost too much to take in: the sweeping lines of the casing, all curves after the straight rule of the keyboard; the gleam of the brass pedals, shaped like some-thing that ought to slip into a shoe, suspended just above floor level. Then there was the satisfaction of propping the hinged lid on its polished stick, revealing the rich interior – cross-hatchings of strings on a frame the colour of old gold, from the fine wires of the high notes to the bass strings almost as fat as earthworms; and the anticipatory pleasure of sitting down to play, adjusting the stool and lifting the keyboard lid to show the keys, the tooth-white naturals and the black tabs of the sharps and flats in their clusters of twos and threes. And at this moment, before ever a hand was lifted and brought down, or a pedal pressed, it was as if you were already hearing the softness of the instrument's tone, its felt-cushioned resonances.

It is impossible for me to detach the image of the piano from that of Mummy playing – either one of the many duets we attempted together, in which she invariably took the bass part, or on her own. She had a special piano-playing expression which involved her mouth and jaw working from side to side, while her eyes darted constantly from the music to the keyboard and back.

E very so often Trinny and I would be taken to the coast, either by Mummy or the au pair – there are pictures of Elisabeth and, later, Eva sitting with us on the sandy beach at Exmouth, a favourite destination easily reached by train from Exeter's Central Station. From as early as I can remember I loved looking at the sea and, even more, being on it in a boat. On the beach at Exmouth there was a gangway of planks attached to two large wheels which could be pushed into the water, allowing passengers to embark on sturdy open motor boats for trips round the bay. They went as far as Orcombe Point, at the eastern edge of the town, and far enough out to round a large bell-buoy which rolled and heaved on the slightest swell, setting the clapper going and producing a doleful tolling.

In Exeter we were allowed to roam more widely as we got a bit older, but only when we knew our telephone number by heart and promised to ring if ever we were delayed or in difficulty. Or we were to ask a policeman for help. This was possible up to a point, but policemen could be forbidding, their height exaggerated by the tall spike on their helmet. Every so often one would come to the house to check up on the current au pair, which seemed rather intrusive. And once I was told off by one in town for trying to give a penny to a beggar selling matches.

Sometimes Trinny and I would walk together up Stoke Hill, at the end of our road past the tennis courts. The road soon turned into a country lane, with overarching trees and high hedges from which we could pick primroses and ragged robin to bring back for Mummy as an already wilting bouquet. At the other end of the road, crossing over Pennsylvania Road and passing the County Cricket Ground, there was Hoopern Valley to explore. A steep field led down to a shallow stream closed in by trees and tangled undergrowth where you could not be seen, and only speckles of sunlight filtered through. It felt risky, but agreeably so. There were dams to make, and trees which had fallen across the water to balance on. All the same, I don't think either of us would have gone there without the other.

Further afield there was Belmont Park, where the playground had a seriously tall slide and swings that went so high they took your breath away. And Heavitree Gardens, where the swings were more manageable, but where there was sometimes a man who softly sang 'Put another nickel in, in old Charlie's nickel tin', and whom we instinctively kept clear of.

Sometimes we would play on the bombsites opposite the Odeon, with their patina of brickdust, where buddleia and stonecrop were making the most of plentiful opportunities for colonisation. The bombsites seemed to remain for a long time, though further down towards the city centre tall hoardings went up to cover the most obvious derelictions, propped up with wooden buttresses like studio façades.

Slowly, things were on the move. Ambitious plans had been laid for the rebuilding of the city and published in a book, *Exeter Phoenix*, in which the drawings seemed as glossy and futuristic as the world inhabited by Dan Dare in the *Eagle*. One bird for another. But it would take more than drawings to cure the city of the fogs, encouraged by coal fires, which enveloped it from time to time. Then, everything became guesswork. Though there was little traffic and pedestrians were few, the traffic lights and Belisha beacons kept on working: faint blobs of cherry, amber and emerald, and madly occulting orange domes. Occasionally a double-decker bus would loom up, spectral as a seaside pier that had broken loose and was adrift on an ebb tide. Down by the river, the fog was even more opaque: one year it obliterated almost completely the lights of the fair which had set up close to the gasholders at the far end of the quay.

Next to the still roofless market in Queen Street, the sense of post-war renewal was marked by the triumphant visit of the Vienna Boys' Choir to the Civic Hall. Watching these beings with their dark blue sailor suits and perfectly parted hair, and hearing the acidic purity of their voices, I thought that they looked wonderfully handsome and grown-up: yet what I most felt was a foolish sense of envy, a certainty that theirs was a charmed world I could never enter.

The Theatre Royal, narrowly spared by the bombs, also re-opened with a flourish, and the improbable portly figure of Cliff Gwilliam, its manager, was to be seen armed with a Churchillian cigar, at the top of the steps, beneath the slightly rickety wooden hoarding bearing the title of the current show. Behind him, the likes of A. E. Matthews or Elsie and Doris Waters came and went.

Along the road, someone else had bought a car. It stood near the corner shop, black and shiny as a pair of army boots, its bonnet fronted by a blue, red and silver globe.

*

Perhaps Devonians were right in what they said about for-eigners. Though we were happily settled, we still looked to London, thinking of it as the centre of our world, a view encouraged by Mummy. London was where the most exciting expeditions and the biggest treats happened: and the excitement began with the journey there, on the Torbay Express, and lunch in the restaurant car as the first treat. At the risk of sounding like an entry in one of Mummy's travel logs, I must record that nowhere else could match the floury mock turtle or Windsor soup to be had on that train.

When you got there, there was no end to the wonders – as a prime instance, theatre matinées at which tea was brought to your seat in the interval, in white cups of thick earthenware, with a pot to match. One of the most memorable plays was *Peter Pan* at the Scala, with Margaret Lockwood as the eternal boy, though it was somehow puzzling that Mr Darling and Captain Hook were played by the same actor. There was much else: travel in black taxis or, better still, our maternal grandparents' hired Daimler, to the Carlton Grill; huge department stores; the underground with its moving stairs; and, very occasionally, a short stay with our grandparents at their flat in Kensington, at Campden Hill Gate. There it felt and smelt opulent. Unlike home, it had fitted carpets and central heating, and there was a floorboard in the hallway which, by creaking softly when you walked on it, inexplicably added to the sense of luxury. In an umbrella stand inside the front door there was also my grandfather's dress sword, huge in its scabbard.

Even approaching the flat was an excitement of its own: pulling open the first black iron gate to the lift in the hall, with its highly polished brass handle, then pushing aside the second concertina gate and stepping into the lift itself. It wobbled slightly as you did so, the way a boat does when you get into it.

Time actually spent with the grandparents was more problematical. True, there was a television in a large mahogany casing, on which we were allowed to watch 'Muffin the Mule', but there was also, on at least one occasion, a wardress hired to organise us and keep us in order. Trinny and I were marched by her to the Victoria and Albert Museum and made to take some sort of interest in the Great Bed of Ware, among other things, though by the time we returned we were so weary and footsore that any bed would have done. In any case we were made to lie on our beds each afternoon, with the curtains drawn.

Paddie could be highly amusing and quite daring, as it seemed to us: on one occasion she threw oranges across the table at dinner; on another, lettuce coated with white pepper. She could be very generous, if she felt like it; at the same time, even at our age we could tell that she was tricky. Our return home was usually followed by some disparaging comment: once Mummy was mortified by being told that her children had dirty ears, and took this as a terrible judgement on her. She may have recalled only too clearly her mother's earlier views on twins.

For me, nothing could spoil the pleasure of being taken by my grandfather to sail my model yacht on the Round Pond in Kensington Gardens. He was endlessly patient, and when the yacht got stuck in the middle of the pond, he quickly found someone to retrieve it. His whole manner was mild, like his smile. He never hurried you, or made you feel a nuisance. His nickname, 'Lucy', never explained, seemed to convey something of his inherent sweetness. He gave me a miniature flag with the arms of the Honourable Artillery Company, of the kind worn in a lapel or used to decorate a formal dinner setting, to fly from the masthead of my yacht.

Seen even more rarely than my grandparents was Uncle Basil, though wherever in the world his film-making took him he diligently sent us postcards, often with spectacular stamps. This gave him a kind of magic aura well justified when we did meet him. He used an electric razor and shaved in bed, a phenomenon doubly novel to us. The lotion which he dabbed onto his face afterwards from a little glass bottle was an interesting pale yellow colour and smelt like perfume. He was the owner of a portable radio. He made early morning tea and would offer us some in delicate Indian Tree cups. He was tall, and dressed elegantly. He had brown suede shoes.

It was Basil, too, who took me to the Festival of Britain, indulging me wildly at the funfair in Battersea Park by allowing me to go on the dodgems no less than thirteen times. This orgy of collisions, along with the ghost train and the big dipper, seemed much more exciting than either the Dome of Discovery or the Skylon on the South Bank. I was not, however, allowed to go on the Wall of Death.

We had no idea then of the distinction our uncle had achieved as a documentary film-maker, and he had the same kind of natural modesty as his father, which would have prevented him from enlightening us. Only later did we learn of his place in the documentary film movement and his work as producer, director or co-director of films such as *Song of Ceylon, Night Mail, World without End* and *The Waters of Time*.

*

If expeditions to London were infrequent, even rarer was the journey north to visit our aunt Peggy, who was married to a man considerably older than herself, Francis Cave, a widower. They lived in a grand house in the Wirral, Woodhey, where Mummy first took us in the summer of 1950. I have a vague memory of a long wait for a connecting train at Crewe.

Crewe, said Mummy, was a junction, as if this somehow explained it.

Woodhey harboured a magic of its own – as well as the spaciousness of the house and the surrounding garden and shrubbery, there was a Jersey cow called Bess, a pig or two and a scatter of chickens. More swallows than we had ever seen swooped in and out under the eaves of the cowshed. We spent a lot of time watching the animals, when we were not making nuisances of ourselves by pushing the revolving summerhouse round and round at a speed which cannot have been good for it. Trinny became so obsessed by the cow Bess that for some time after we got home she insisted on wandering round the back lawn on all fours, with slippers on her hands and a dressing-gown cord as a tail. She developed a quite convincing moo.

Uncle Francis, who worked for and eventually presided over the Mersey Dock and Harbour Board, drove a large beige Austin that smelt of leather. It had a large A on its bonnet, with horizontal strips of metal going back from the letter to suggest fleetness. Uncle Francis could be prevailed upon to drive at speed over a humpbacked bridge near the house, producing a terrific sinking in the stomach. He also drove us more than once through the road tunnel under the Mersey. When not in use, the Austin was kept in a large garage piled to the roof with bales of straw on which you could play for hours, from time to time falling down a level or two between bales, and finally retiring to the house hot and prickly, with dust in your hair.

Peggy, unable to have children of her own after an operation on her stomach, combined a sense of fun with a no-nonsense attitude. A convert to Roman Catholicism, her husband's faith, she took us with her when she went aboard a Cunard liner in the docks, to change the altar frontal in the ship's chapel. We were given tea with the captain, and a whole heap of menus from the dining room to take away with us. But what really put us in awe of our aunt was the way in which she could shuffle cards by splicing two packs together at speed, pulling her lips back in a grimace and screwing up her eyes as she did so, as if the whole business were causing her acute pain.

*

It is hard to judge how difficult we were as small children, particularly given Mummy's combination of tolerance and the setting of standards. Once, at Christmas, she must have feared that the tolerance had gone too far, and adopted what she thought would be an ingenious way of inducing a little humility. She told us that if we had been naughty during the year Father Christmas would bring us not just gifts, but lumps of coal which would, of course, take up some of the room that might otherwise have been available for presents.

On Christmas morning I woke early, as every child does, to the promising rustle and heaviness of the stocking across the bottom of the bed. To my chagrin, by the time I had excavated it down to the toe I had discovered several lumps of coal, wrapped in newspaper. I felt deeply ashamed, and made haste to hide them in the drawer with my handkerchiefs, before Trinny or Mummy came in.

Breakfast was not quite the occasion it was meant to be. I was much too cheerful, and Trinny much too downcast. Finally, Mummy asked her what the matter was, where-upon she burst into tears: oh, she had sinned, she had been naughty, and there was coal in her stocking to prove it. She was inconsolable. My mother turned to ask me whether I, too, had found coal in my stocking. No, really not, no, none at all, I answered. Here was a conundrum for her, only to be resolved when, later, she found the stuff hidden under my once clean handkerchiefs and could confront me with the evidence. But she might have reflected that my shame was obviously as great as Trinny's distress.

*

The only Christmas we spent with our grandparents and Uncle Basil was memorable for better reasons. At one time they owned a lovely old timber-framed house at Rolphy Green, in Essex near Pleshey. The ambient temperature made Union Road seem warm by comparison, but it did have seats inside the large fireplace where you could easily get too warm. The rest of the place, draughty enough upstairs for screens to have been put up, seemed arctic by comparison. When we were there the weather was very cold. I remember a wonderful night-time walk, under a moon not far off the full, on a flat lane which ran between fields of sugar beet sparkling with frost.

It was at Rolphy that we were given our first bicycles. Does any child forget that moment? Mine was a metallic green, and Trinny's a shiny blue. I don't know whether such things as stabilisers existed then, but if so we didn't have the benefit of them. Much of our time was spent wobbling uncertainly across the lawn, Uncle Basil starting us off with enough momentum for us to begin to balance. Sooner or later we would lose control and crash into one of the tall standard roses which stood at intervals. By the time we left, with a fair number of scratches and thorn splinters, we had begun to get the hang of it.

At school, I had reached the age limit for boys. The time had come to exchange the navy blue and yellow of Edgerton Park for the maroon and blue of Norwood, a preparatory school only about half a mile further away, almost at the bottom of the long slope of Pennsylvania Road. The school had been going for some time, at least since the 1920s. It took a small number of boarders as well as day boys. The accommodation was rather cramped and, though there was a green space behind the school, most games took place on grounds owned by the University, about ten minutes' walk away.

The headmaster, C. J. B. Robinson, was in every respect a towering figure, whose authority could not be doubted and was rarely, if ever, challenged. If it was, he had no compunction about having recourse to the cane. Said to be a retired coffee planter whose work had been in Malaya, he managed to give the impression of walking with magisterial uprightness and, at the same time, in a rather hunched way, perhaps to keep in place the rather frayed black book (a bible?) he carried about clamped under one arm. Sallow and wrinkled in complexion, he had a sharp nose like an owl's beak, and crinkly dark hair beginning to go thin. The force of his sarcasm could reduce a boy to pulp at a range co-terminous with earshot, but there was a twinkle in his eyes with their attendant crow's-feet, and the smile was not invariably sardonic, though with inattentive pupils he was fond of producing it while quoting Christ's pronouncement on Lazarus: 'He is not dead, but sleepeth.'

His two great interests were Latin, which he taught to the top forms, and sport. In the case of the former, his great allies were rain and a steady hand: homework done badly resulted in the offender's exercise book being frisbeed across the classroom in the direction of a window sportingly left open a little at the top, thus allowing at least the possibility that it might not fall outside. It was not clear whether this amounted to a first lesson in the role of chance in life, or was merely a way of the headmaster amusing himself. Wet weather added a sharper dimension since, if it did fall outside, the book could not be retrieved until the bell went for the end of the lesson. History does not relate (another favourite phrase of his) whether this system promoted greater diligence among the pupils, though it was certainly the case that most parts of *Kennedy's Latin Primer*, including the principal ones, were well ingested, as the traditional schoolboy emendation of 'Latin' to 'Eating' suggested they could be. Robbie liked to urge his pupils to 'read, mark, learn and inwardly digest'.

Nothing, however, could match Robbie's driving enthusiasm for sport, particularly cricket and football. Since I was not much good at cricket ('keen but erratic', read my first report, a really rather kindly estimate), I did not come across Robbie much in that context, though I saw him bowl impressively in the nets. But I did in time experience the full rigour of his love of football. For him, success on the field was as crucial for the honour of the school as defeat was detrimental to it, and he worked at training and drilling the 1st XI with unrelenting zeal. The effects of his labours reverberated right through the school, and fixtures against other teams were undertaken with gladiatorial savagery, particularly in the case of Bramdean, Norwood's rival school in Exeter. The savagery was intensified by the primitive nature of the equipment. Football boots were gnarled and knobbly things, not unlike Gertrude Jekyll's gardening boots, turning up at the toes and with heavy studs made of rounds of layered leather impaled on glinting silvery nails. These, when exposed by wear, could inflict a considerable gash on an opponent's leg. The ball itself, sturdily constructed of panels of leather stitched together, was difficult enough to bring under control at the best of times. In wet weather it became about as heavy as a ballista rock, and could jar every tooth in your jaw if you were foolish enough to attempt to head it. Football matches also seemed to take place in a seeping micro-climate of their own, on murky fields where the rain swept across and the cold rose wetly through your feet. A draggled crew of bellicose fathers stormed restlessly up and down the touchline, shouting angry encouragement.

The Deputy Head, Mr Layton, taught English and was altogether different. His mild disposition was sometimes taken for weakness, and it was true that he didn't quite have Robbie's ability to maintain an iron grip, though he did have the gift of being able to raise one eyebrow a long way. I liked him, and when he could make himself heard above the noise of insubordination he was sympathetic and encouraging. His wife, who had much to do with the boarding side, was altogether more forceful and not to be crossed, though on the rare occasions when she was free of the pressures of her job she, too, could be kindly. She presented a strong contrast to Robbie's wife, an apparently timid person who was rarely seen and said to be ill.

The rest of the staff was a richly varied collection, from the very good to the well intentioned to the downright psychopathic. One teacher in particular was renowned for his sudden and violent losses of temper, which would propel him in a frenzy across the room at speed. Noisily knocking over any furniture in his way, he would grab whoever had ignited his ire by the hair, which he then shook mercilessly, removing whole tufts when he was really incensed. Another had an Adam's apple so prominent that it looked like a real obstruction which every breath and word had to get round. It rose and fell alarmingly. One boy swore that it was a deadly illness: the thing would grow bigger and bigger until it killed him. Mr Bainbridge, who taught maths and collected stamps, seemed to have been dipped into a vat of talcum powder or, more likely, chalk. His white hair, along with the smoke rising from his pipe, heightened the impression of a soft cloud brought to earth.

Occasionally there would be a teacher who came to the school but left abruptly, a discreet veil being drawn over the reasons for his departure. Apart from Miss Beckett and Miss Baker, who taught the bottom two forms, all the staff were male.

As well as the more usual subjects, Greek was offered for boys requiring it for entrance to their next school, and there were various other extras such as piano lessons and carpentry, the latter taught by Mr Bayles in the Nissen hut overlooking the asphalt playground. A rather tense person who always wore a brown overall, Mr Bayles learnt, long before GCSE coursework, how to patrol skilfully the border between the pupils' own efforts and a helping hand. The other use of the Nissen hut was for lectures and films, with rudimentary but quite effective blackout pinned across the windows.

Hymns, sung daily from a green book, played a surprisingly large part in things, not so much individually but in terms of the context they created, a world not dissimilar to that of the Pathé News, one in which, eventually, all manner of things would be well. Some situations already seemed fine as they were: the spicy breezes of Java's isle or, for that matter, Greenland's icy mountains and India's coral strands. On the other hand, there was that thick darkness brooding yet o'er heathen lands afar, waiting for the oncoming morning star. Then there was the fair waving of the golden corn in Canaan's pleasant land, spread out beneath the spacious firmament on high, where the spangled heavens suggested the bonus of confectionery. True, there was the world's tempestuous sea to navigate, but there was good cheer too, notably in the happy band of pilgrims and the rousing onwardness of Christian soldiers. Not even the sombre servitude of forty days and forty nights in the wild seemed too terrible, on the face of it, and the sacred head sore wounded sounded like quite a mild affliction, as a sore head would be. That left Mrs Alexander's green hill and 'Away in a manger', which also always filled me with dread and a sense of desolation, though I have no idea why.

For the moment all this lay ahead of me, as it did for the four little wooden figures representing the four houses to one of which every pupil belonged (Greeks, Trojans, Romans and Vikings), which were moved up long ladders in the classroom used for assemblies, according to a complicated points system. I began in Form 2, the empire of Miss Baker. Here, not unlike people undergoing some sort of rehabilitation, we stitched cards which already had animal shapes pricked out in holes, and made things from raffia or from a grid that you threaded with wool. My mother kept a needle holder made by this method until her death.

An early alarm sounded in the form of small bottles of

milk, each holding a third of a pint, which were distributed to all pupils at break-time. I was able to gain an exemption by bringing a letter from Mummy explaining that I was allergic to the white stuff.

Not long after the arrival of their still-born daughter, my parents moved out of London. My mother always said that this was to get away from the Blitz, but perhaps it was also to help overcome their grief and make what could be seen as a new start.

They either rented or bought Tillerton, a small farm set on its own in the swooping hill country between Crediton and Tedburn St Mary, about ten miles west of Exeter. The farmhouse itself was a low building more like a cottage, with roses growing over the small thatched porch.

It was a mixed holding, with sheep, pigs and some arable. Daddy was practical and could turn his hand to almost anything, but neither he nor Mummy ever talked much about this time, and all that has come down is the odd anecdote. Whether the idea was to make a modest living, or simply to subsist, is not clear. In any case, in January 1942 Mummy became pregnant again, and it was decided to call upon the services of the same London gynaecologist as before. Other than bad morning sickness there were no complications, and Trinny and I were born at St Mary's Hospital, Paddington, on a late October morning. My mother used to say proudly that we were the first set of twins to be born in what she always called the 'new' Lindo wing, but given that the building had been completed four years earlier, this seems improbable, unless there was a sudden national dearth of twins.

Over the next four years the marriage fell apart. Little light is shed by such stories as exist, for example the one about my father falling off a white horse, drunkenly, on his way back from The King's Arms in Tedburn one winter night, and lying for some time in the snow. Much later Mummy related, as a casual matter of fact, an occasion when Daddy came down the drive firing a shotgun, though why was not explained. Perhaps he handed on to me a proneness to mishaps, since I managed to notch up quite a tally while we were at Tillerton. I fell through the bottom of a pram, having jumped too hard in it. I got my fingers stuck in an electric plug and, on another occasion, in the orchard I rocked our double pram sufficiently to displace the stone put under the wheel to back up a weak brake. The pram with both of us in it jolted at speed all the way down a steep slope, luckily remaining upright: a Devonian version of the pram careering down the Odessan flight of steps in the film *Battleship Potemkin*. More seriously, while sitting in the kitchen on the lap of a land girl, I managed to pull down onto myself a large kettle filled with boiling water. That meant hospital in Exeter, where I failed to thrive because, my mother alleged, they called me by my middle name of Richard, which I simply didn't know and therefore did not respond to. The hospital warned my parents that I was not doing well. They decided – against the advice of the professionals – to take me home, where I recovered. I still bear the evidence of this accident, in the form of skin grafts on my left forearm, but can recall nothing of it beyond a vague memory of a dressing-gown soaked with boiling water and clinging to me like the shirt of Nessus.

*

Our parents had very little to say to us about what went wrong between them. Mummy always maintained that the

71

war was to blame and left it at that. How this could have been so was not clear, especially as but for the war and the events leading up to it our parents would almost certainly not have met, but further enquiries were not invited. Once or twice she let slip that Daddy had been rather too fond of his drink and his girlfriends. At any rate, it seems clear that she felt insufficiently loved and, ultimately, betrayed, though this is the kind of dramatic word she would never have used. Daddy once told me wryly that he had not expected Mummy to walk out, as she did. On the very few occasions that Trinny and I saw them together, there was never any acrimony: perhaps it was all too long over for that. Instead, there was a curious formality informed by affection. Daddy would always bow to Mummy and, as part of the same forward inclination, take her hand and kiss it.

Only the moment of their severance has survived, as a story which, in its detail at least, may owe as much to myth as to history. Returning to Tillerton (from where? At what time of the day or night?), Daddy found that Mummy had gone (a note on the kitchen table, or on the dressing-table in the bedroom? Did she say where she was going?), taking the children with her. Panicking, he seized the only remaining member of the household, the aged and purblind cocker spaniel Sally, and made off to Exeter in pursuit of his wife. Attempting to board a train at the city's Central Station, he became entangled in the dog's lead and fell headlong into a compartment at the feet, and the shapely legs, of a W.R.A.F. radar operator called Dolores whom, it transpired, he had met before somewhere. To her he poured out his heart and, in the fullness of time, much else. Our half-sister Amata was born in the summer of 1946.

Years later, after Daddy's death, a piece of paper slid out of one of his books, *La Folie de Van Gogh*. On it, in a large, quite bold sloping hand, was written the name Amata Brown, with an address in Cassis: black ink faded to sepia. Too late by then to know what significance it might have had, if any.

Now I was allowed to go and watch Exeter City by myself. Worming my way to the front of the open terraces behind one of the goals, I soaked it all up: the bright green jersey of the goalkeeper called, I think, Kelly; the figure of the midfield player Arnie Mitchell, tall and close to bald (a result, I thought, of heading the ball too much); the shouts of 'Up the City!', or 'Windy!' when the opposition passed back; the dry clacking of rattles; the rare triumph of a goal. Peripheral events were just as thrilling: the railway band which played before the match, with their bright silver euphoniums and tubas, and the high-pitched slender horn produced with a flourish for the Post Horn Gallop; the man wearing a kilt and balancing a large dolls' house on his head, who went round the pitch at half-time collecting for charity; the kiosk in one of the stands from which you could buy crisps with bits of green on them and the taste of seaweed. And every so often a train would rush by, invisible in its deep cutting, but sending up a bluff of steam and always shrieking a whistle blast.

Even here an Austrian angle managed to infiltrate, with a visiting team taking on the home side one evening under the recently installed floodlights. Marian, Mummy and I sat high up in the covered stand, my mother very pleased for some reason by the fact that the Austrians' shirts were old gold. We sat there staring out at the rain teeming down. I don't know who won. And where was Trinny?

*

Marian became a more enigmatic presence than ever. Astonishingly, Trinny and I still had no real idea of how things were between him and Mummy. We never heard dissent, but then we rarely witnessed affection. Did they think it best to keep it like that for fear of hurting our feelings, or was there some other explanation? There are times when adults, too, are seen but not heard.

People of various ages, ostensibly relatives of his, came to stay briefly and went away again. Among them was a boy called Tony, very red in the face and with curly fair hair, a bit older than us. He seemed very upset and burst into tears at supper. Then there was a young woman called Rixie or Trixie, again fair, very pretty and with an attractive necklace at the top of her white blouse. She smiled a lot. Cousins? Nephew and niece? Son and daughter, even? Trinny and I looked on baffled, wondering who was who and why they were behaving as they did. One day a middle-aged woman arrived, dressed in black and with a gold tooth as prominent as Mr Hornung's. She announced in a foreign accent (German? Austrian? Somewhere else?) that she was Mrs Marian. We had no idea what this was about, either, though she was angry about something.

Marian himself was increasingly unwell. He would sit at the end of the dining-table, racked by a painful smoker's cough which made his eyes water, and bringing up terrible gobbets of phlegm which, if he could, he would smuggle into a handkerchief before anyone could see them. The whites of his eyes had become a dull yellow; the eyes seemed to protrude more than they had.

At some point he took to his bed, and a sickroom unease descended on the household. Finally, one morning, a large black ambulance drew up in the road outside. With its great silver hinges on the back doors, it looked almost like a hearse. As Trinny and I watched from the edge of the path going down to the back garden, we saw a gleaming chrome stretcher with little wheels being carried into the house. Some time later Marian was borne down the front steps, strapped in and under a red blanket. There was something awful about it. We continued to look on, appalled and fascinated, as they slid him into the dark.

The year 1952 started so well, with a Saturday early in the year mesmerising all of us in the Odeon audience. On the screen, a badly listing ship bucked and swooped violently in a swollen sea. It banged down onto the waves, lifted its screw clear, slewed from one great trough to the next. Two tiny figures clung to the aft rail. The confident Pathé voice told us cheerfully that this was a stricken American cargo ship, the *Flying Enterprise* ('stricken' was definitely a Pathé word) which had been adrift in the Atlantic for six days and nights with only her skipper, Captain Kurt Carlsen, aboard. An American destroyer had stood by, but all attempts to get a line on board the freighter had been defeated by the severe weather. Then the British salvage tug *Turmoil* had come to help, its first mate making a daring leap onto the stern of the *Flying Enterprise* and so ending the captain's lonely vigil. In the end, though, it proved impossible to take the vessel in tow. To an obbligato of rousing music we saw the two tiny figures leaping into the sea and being picked up. The cargo ship finally slid down beneath the waves. Then, shots of the gallant captain ('gallant', another Pathé word) cheerfully drinking cocoa as *Turmoil* headed for her home port of Falmouth and a civic welcome.

This was classic newsreel footage, in which danger is overcome or at least mitigated thanks to the intervention of the British (forget that American destroyer standing by) and a good time is, in the end, had by almost everyone. In such a world surely nothing could go fundamentally wrong.

Yet within a month everything had gone wrong. When King George VI died early in February, the wireless and newsreel voices turned solemn, and the music slowed. The newspaper headlines went thick and black; flags appeared, flown at half-mast. We were made to feel that there was something outrageous about the striking down of a monarch who was also a friend – the loveable man who at the end had so simply been taken a cup of morning tea, one he would never drink.

Miles of newsprint were devoted to appreciations of the late king, in particular his part in sustaining the nation in wartime. Then there were all the details of the dying, such as the coffin being made of strong oak by carpenters at Sandringham, where the king had died, and the story of how the young princess, his daughter, had gone up into a tree in Kenya as herself, and come down a queen.

At Norwood, on the day of the funeral, the entire school assembled. A large wireless had been set up on a stool, connected by a curling length of purple flex to the ceiling light with its white bakelite shade. The wireless itself had been draped with a square of black cotton, secured as if it were a wimple. Solemn music came forth.

There was no question of being allowed to sit. All through the proceedings – the barked commands, the funeral marches, the crackling of the gun carriage wheels on the road surface, the clopping of hooves, the jingle of harness – we had to stand in silence. The hushed tones of the commentator, his words spoken so close to the microphone that they sounded furtive, reminded us of the depth of the grief we were to feel. Sometimes, between rituals, there was no sound other than the hissing atmospheric of the wireless. By the time the procession had left Hyde Park, swinging left to enter the Edgware Road, our grief was becoming distorted by discomfort. When we had reached St George's Chapel, Windsor, and while the Archbishop of Canterbury was intoning the liturgy of the funeral service, one boy in the room fainted. This was, however, dealt with sympathetically, almost reverentially, as if he had blessedly produced the stigmata on Good Friday.

At last it was nearly over. We heard the Lord Chamberlain snap his staff, and the commentator told us that the queen was scattering a few grains of red earth from a silver bowl onto the coffin. The wireless relayed someone unexpectedly shouting 'God save the queen!' and shortly afterwards we were released, to trail home.

*

At home, things were worse than we knew. Accusations had been made against Marian by a newspaper, *The People*, alleging that he was a con man and a fraudster. Marian had sued for libel: damagingly, the jury had been unable to agree. From what Mummy said later, there may have been a retrial, with the jury again hung.

Marian's illness, diagnosed as lung cancer, was protracted. Trinny and I were sent to stay with Aunty Peggy in Cheshire: kind as she was, it seemed a long stay. Marian lingered on in a nursing home in St John's Wood, with my mother nursing him. He died in the middle of April. We made a banner of welcome for my mother's return, stretching it across the drive at Woodhey: bright Indian inks which had a pungent smell, and ran.

After Marian's death, though we did not know it at the time, my mother as executrix was threatened with litigation by his family, who claimed an interest in the estate. This hung over her for several years, though it is typical of her that she told us nothing of it till much later.

*

At some point in the year Eva left to marry her boyfriend Ray, who was in the marines. We missed her, not just for her humour and her cooking, but for the help she gave us in all sorts of ways. For me this included taking advantage of her considerable skills in calligraphy and drawing. Who would do my copybook writing now? And how could I ever hope to match the beautiful maps she handed in for my geography prep, with the coastlines neatly fringed in blue?

Our last au pair was, predictably, a let-down by comparison. Isolde was German, not Austrian, the daughter of the owner of a sausage factory in the Black Forest, according to Mummy. She was pallid and never wore make-up. What she lacked by way of a sense of humour she did not really compensate for in other respects, we thought, in the way of making judgements that children have. When it did come to humour, her idea of a joke was to stand at the top of the house and yell for Mummy. When she, always easily alarmed and perhaps thinking back to my night-time cries from the same quarter a few years before, called back to ask what the matter was, Isolde would announce cheerfully, 'It is nothing, Mrs Sail. It is a joke!' Maybe it was the way she told them.

Isolde acquired an Egyptian boyfriend, Aziz, a postgraduate who lived quite close to Norwood, and she would often pop out to see him, saying with a peculiar sing-song intonation and a predominance of 'z' sounds that she was 'going to help Aziz with his theziz'.

When Isolde left – I don't think she can have stayed for

very long, and perhaps she also went off to marry – her legacy was a handsome cuckoo clock with heavy weights in the form of fir cones, and a cuckoo which really knew its business. There was something especially pleasing about the way in which the little door flew open on the hour and the bird came out to tell the time, bobbing and even opening and closing its beak.

I hope we thanked her properly.

*

By the time Pathé brought us pictures of the Lynton floods in August, it seemed that not much else was left to go wrong. The commentator had lost his customary hectoring ebullience, and even the accompanying music, swirling like the muddy floodwaters as they bore boulders, trees and anything else in their path down to the sea, just sounded grim.

M ummy had a chameleon-like capacity for adaptation: in fact, could probably have done nothing to prevent it. This was both a strength and a weakness. It made her, for instance, an ideal travelling companion. It also enabled her to sympathise with others and look at things from their point of view. This in turn made her blind to many social distinctions, such as class, though like anyone she had the limitations of her generation and her upbringing. It also gave her spontaneity, and single-mindedness in pursuing objectives. On the other hand, it also meant that she put all her eggs in one basket at any given time. This was particularly the case with relationships: she would adopt the style, the speech patterns and even to some extent the outlook of those she was currently close to, sometimes to the exclusion of others.

The most enduring aspect of her single-mindedness was, of course, her obsession with Austria. Some people feel that they have been born with the wrong gender: Mummy might have felt the same about her nationality. If there had been such an operation as a transpatriotomy, she might well have opted for it.

What we failed to discern, through the assorted murks of 1952 (and were too young anyway to realise), was the extent to which things were about to change. It wasn't that Mummy had neglected us: but now, with Marian gone and the buffer zone constituted by the au pair girls no longer in existence, it was we who could occupy the forefront of her attention. No doubt this also had something to do with the simple fact that we were older and perhaps better company. But the single-mindedness remained, and for at least one twin this could not be good. Perhaps for both.

Spending more time with Mummy, we began to know her better: and the new situation made demands on all of us. Much remained unchanged, of course, such as her gift for mimicry, or the way she could make us laugh by waggling her eyebrows or twitching the end of her nose – that nose which dripped impressively when she caught a bad cold, as she frequently did. Her colds, in fact, brought out two conflicting sides of her character: a dogged persistence which went uneasily along with a sense of grievance, injustice almost. It was the same when she found herself in a queue, where she could be as competitive as she was on the tennis court. Aware that at five foot four she might have to defend her patch, if anyone should accidentally jostle her she would give them an instant hostile glare and, sometimes, stagger about in an exaggerated fashion as if the offender had launched a deliberate attack on her. She had also become convinced, no doubt as the result of hard experience, that a woman on her own was likely to be slighted, done down or simply ignored. The exaggerated response as a symptom of feeling embattled became habitual as she grew older, extending to situations in which she really had no cause to feel under attack. In old age, when she was a passenger in a car, it only needed an instance of moderately hard braking by the driver for Mummy to react as if she were being bounced from dashboard to window to windscreen and back again.

There were times when we found the degree of anxiety expressed in Mummy's eyes very troubling. She seemed so vulnerable, in her emotional directness, and we dreaded her propensity for weeping at moments of disagreement or minor family conflict. At such times we felt both helpless and horribly guilty, knowing how generous and affectionate she was to us in many ways, and how she always set out to do her very best on our behalf. But this was her whole *modus operandi*, really, a kind of innocence in the face of the world which was not without its own ruthlessness. To see it in the terms of the Scottish poet Edwin Muir's memorable line about 'the hardened old and the hard-hearted young', Mummy never became hardened, while for Trinny and me, as for many children as they grow up, there was no way through to independence without times of hard-heartedness and its concomitant feelings of self-reproach. We barged into her in the queue.

*

Mummy resumed her love affair with the motor car. It was as if, from puberty onwards, her menstrual cycle and the Otto cycle had found themselves in perfect and lasting syn-chronicity. It was Fords that she was most enamoured of, maintaining that they were the best make in every way. She also claimed that they loved the night air, and ran particu-larly well after dark. This was hard to disprove, as was her assertion, if someone commented in summer on the noonday heat, that what made it even more remarkable was that it was only eleven o'clock by the sun.

We didn't have a car of our own and hired one, usually for the day, from a Mr Peachey. He had several Ford Prefects, at least two of them beige and one black, in varying stages of decomposition. The hope was to have the luck to get one which either lasted for the whole day and didn't leave you stranded in the middle of Dartmoor or at the coast, or one which broke down or had its tyre go flat before you were out of the city, when there was a chance that you would be offered another vehicle. Punctures were common, since the tyres on several of the cars were bald. If contacted with the news that there was a problem, Mr Peachey was pretty grumpy and managed to convey the impression that it was the customer's fault. Nevertheless, we had some highly enjoyable outings in these variable vessels, often despite incredibly dim headlights and engines phlegmy with age and the need for decoking. So much so that, flying in the face of common sense, Mummy decided on a longer expedition in the summer of 1953 and drove us up through the Cotswolds to Cheshire, to see Aunty Peggy and Uncle Francis. To everyone's surprise, including Mr Peachey's for all I know, that particular Ford Prefect, one of the beige ones, performed faultlessly.

Unlike the year that it followed, 1953 brought with it a groundswell of optimism further enhanced by the end of sweet rationing and the splendours of the coronation which, it was confidently predicted, would usher in a new Elizabethan age of splendour and accomplishment in every sphere. The ceremony was watched on television by some but not by us, since, like many people, we did not have a set or ready access to one. A special film of it came to the cinema soon enough, in glorious Technicolor, drummers, trumpeters, archbishop and all. The crown looked too big, and I wondered whether, in the midst of all that pomp and circumstance, it might suddenly fall to the ground and roll away. But it didn't, and 'Vivat! Vivat!' cried the Abbey congregation, like a well-rehearsed team cheering the opposition at the end of the match.

It was impossible to remain indifferent to such a spectacle, especially when it was combined with the first ascent of

Everest, by a British team. Well, a sherpa and a New Zealander, but they could be easily subsumed. For Pathé and British Movietone, these were events to induce an ecstasy little short of hysteria, and they made the most of them. For me, they didn't altogether dislodge from my mind the pictures I had seen earlier in the year of Stalin, his copious moustache neatly arranged, lying peacefully in his coffin on a bed of all the available roses in Russia.

It was Trinny who was most moved by the coronation. She was a great admirer of the Royal Family: for her it was the death of Queen Mary, rather than Stalin's, which made March memorable. I found this hard to understand, if only because it seemed improbable that such a brittle structure, pure royal cake-icing from hat to toe, could ever have been fully alive. Trinny was equally baffled by my indifference. She was an avid reader of Pitkin Pictorials, a series of glossy booklets about the Royals. Here she could read how the family's unstinting devotion to its subjects ran through every genera-tion, from Queen Mary to Prince Charles to Princess Anne, with whom she clearly identified. Hadn't Queen Mary com-pleted, over nine years, a carpet which she had presented to the nation (even if, puzzlingly, it was destined for an American collection)? Weren't the young prince and his sister so thoughtful as to give away gladly many of the gifts they received, to children less fortunate than themselves? And now at the very centre, taking over from the king, sat the young queen, to whom her father had passed on the gift of being able to wave to subjects with a hand that could swivel miraculously, as if the wrist had been fitted with a universal joint.

Fired with enthusiasm, Trinny wrote to the princess in advance of her coronation, and was rapturous when a reply came from the palace, with the royal arms on the envelope and a note inside from a lady-in-waiting telling Trinny that the princess had instructed her to write and thank her. Wasn't I impressed, she wanted to know, waving the letter in front of me. I was at the time, but in a brotherly way refused to respond with anything more than a curt grunt.

Trinny's other favourite reading matter included *Heidi*, *Black Beauty* and, above all, stories about the Chalet School or any other girls' boarding school in which the gym mistress might be in league with a bullying prefect, or a secret plot be hatched to sabotage the heroine's performance at a vital skiing contest, and in which everything was in the end happily resolved, the wages of sin being failure. Such a hold had these confections taken on her that she begged to be allowed to go to boarding school herself. A search was initiated by Mummy, with Peggy also consulted, and in the autumn Trinny went off to a south Devon school called Hazeldene, in Salcombe. Beautifully set among trees and overlooking North Sands with, in the distance, a view of the headland beyond the Wolf Rock, the school was presided over jointly by two headmistresses, Miss Sermon and Miss Weatherston. They were an interesting double act, Miss Sermon sturdy and tough, Miss Weatherston elegant, slightly fey and likely to be wearing wafty scarves. One teacher, Miss Bowden, had been at Edgerton Park, but I don't know what part she played, if any, in Trinny's translation to the south coast.

The school blazer was pink, closer in tone to the *Manners Neapolitaner* packets than the Chemico tin. A droop of white catkins adorned the breast pocket above the school motto, *Per Ardua ad Astra*, which it neatly shared with the R.A.F. In the school's case *Ardua* did not involve any public examinations, while the *Astra* were really the Bethlehem star in the east,

87

piety being encouraged, and the winding crocodile of girls on their way to and from the town's church a regular routine. The school also offered Margaret Morris Movement dancing, which seemed to involve wearing short coloured tunics and performing stylised manoeuvres and leaps which any brother would have been likely to find mortally embarrassing.

Far worse than any embarrassment was the gap left by Trinny's absence. Of course it was already clear, as it had been from quite early on, that we had different interests and priorities. Orderliness, for one thing, as proved by the two built-in cupboards in the dining-room where we kept our toys. Trinny's was arranged with improbable neatness, even empty paper bags smoothed out, folded and pressed into a small tidy pile. My cupboard, on the other hand, looked as if it had been filled with the help of a shovel, and the contents then churned. This particular difference was greatly to Trinny's disadvantage, since there was no better way to annoy her than to tip everything out of her cupboard. There was little point in her retaliating: I would just heave everything in again and force the door shut.

We had always taken one another for granted, as siblings do. Now it was very peculiar to turn round and find her not there, and being told that we would still have the holidays together wasn't the same. We had spent so many hours in one another's company, doing nothing in particular, or making our own world. We had put on elementary plays together. We had been frightened together. We had dressed up in each other's clothes, and Mummy had had to pretend that she was fooled. We had been bored together. We had made tents out of our thin cotton bedspreads, and hidden beneath them. We had served each other invisible tea drunk from dolls' cups, and eaten air sandwiches.

Yet the divergences were only natural. Trinny read *Girl* and *School Friend*, and I read *Eagle* and *Beano*; she wanted to be Margot Fonteyn or Pat Smythe, I wanted to go to sea. While she was away in the world of the Chalet School, I was piling through as many Captain Hornblower books as could be found in the City Library. We had our own friends: Trinny used to see a lot of a slight, dark-eyed girl called Grenfel Hurford, and I would go to the house of David Salter, along the road from us, where we would listen to 'Jet Morgan: Journey into Space' or 'The Goon Show', which David found much funnier than I did.

There was something else, too. Both of us were, I think, aware that there was a basic inequality between us, about which we could do nothing, though it made me feel guilty, just as it must have been depressing for Trinny. It was as if she were dogged by difficulty and misfortune, while for me things worked out more easily. It was Trinny who took longer to do things; Trinny who put a large garden fork through her foot, having to stand rooted to the spot (the French *clouée sur place* describes it more exactly) while I ran to get help; Trinny who managed to fall, somehow, down the narrow stairwell from the very top of the house, saved only by managing to grasp a narrow iron bar on the way down; Trinny whose teeth seemed liable to crumble on contact with anything harder than egg. Somehow, sharing the long-established family ineptitude for maths, as we did, could not make up for much of this.

Not that I entirely escaped some close brushes with calamity. A close runner-up to the incident with the boiling kettle that landed me in hospital was the time when, speeding recklessly down Pennsylvania on my bike and attempting to turn left into Union Road, I came off and ended up more or less on the bonnet of a car. Then there was the bright morning when I decided to climb out of my bedroom window, right at the top of the house, and stand on the window sill. It was a sash window and I could pull it down quite a way, enough to be able to straddle it. Luckily I was spotted by Mr Isaac, who ran the nursery garden opposite. He rang my mother, who then had to come up and, without alarming me by her sudden arrival, coax me in. Stout horizontal iron bars were subsequently screwed into place across my window, in case I should think to try the trick again. And across Trinny's window, for good measure.

At about this time, I came home after school one afternoon and, still wearing my mud-caked football kit, fainted in the kitchen. I can still remember the way in which the room seemed to slip up and away from me, rather than me sliding down. I managed to avoid banging my head on the kitchen table as I went. This periodic keeling over, relatively infrequently and without any particular warning, has continued.

*

As a family, our closest friends were the Keens, whom we had got to know over the previous year or so. Jane was divorced from her husband Stuart, but had remained on amicable terms with him. She lived with her two children, Nicholas and Sara, at The Old Post Office in Marsh Green, a village close to Exeter. Nicholas was exactly our age, and Sara a little younger. Jane was a remarkable person – highly knowledgeable about theatre and film, with a great sense of humour and an innate shrewdness. She was savvy in a way Mummy certainly wasn't. She eked out a living as best she could, partly by acting as chauffeuse and companion to her great aunt Ethel, who lived in comfortable misery in an

Exeter hotel, weighing her food at the table on a pair of scales and showing every sign of going on for ever. Jane and my mother must been a considerable support to each other, given the similarity of their situations, both with husbands who had remarried, and both with a girl and a boy to bring up.

Nicholas was at school at The Beacon, in Teignmouth, while Sara went to The Maynard in Exeter, so there was no question of meeting at school. But the four of us became good friends and were often together.

We had met their father before, when he was booked to show some films at a children's party. Now that we could get to know him better, we could begin to understand just what a fantastical life he led. At a time when very few people had television, and the H-shaped aerials were a rarity even in towns, Stuart went all round the country showing films which were, many of them, classics or rarities. Any map illustrating the range of his activities would have had to cover the whole of England, and to have been on a large enough scale to show village halls, meeting rooms, memorial institutes, school assembly halls and church annexes, as well as Norwood's own Nissen hut. There, I and my contemporaries thrilled to such unforgettable highlights as *A Christmas Carol*, Olivier's *Henry V* (those flights of arrows!), *Scott of the Antarctic*, *Great Expectations* and – this was almost too exciting to cope with – *Night Mail*, co-directed by Uncle Basil, with verse by Auden and music by Britten.

Apart from anything else, Stuart's life involved incredibly hard work. It often meant driving long distances, for a start, in a grey Ford van (ah, another Ford) which looked more like a battleship of some sort than a road vehicle. You would always know when it was coming. First, you heard the thick,

91

throaty burr of the engine, then you saw the two grey torpedo tubes welded to the roof rack, in which heavy, wood-framed screens lay rolled up. The tubes advanced towards you like lances wielded by jousting knights. Then came the whole square rocking bulk of the van. I see it lifting out of the shimmer of summer air, cresting the rise of a Devon lane thick with cow parsley, in late May: and there, his hair swept back from his broad, sloping forehead, knuckles showing pale along the top of the steering wheel, is Stuart.

It was pure wonder when we went with him, as we quite often did, sometimes the four of us children, sometimes one or two of us. The pattern was basically invariable. The drive, then arrival at the venue, where devotees – and Stuart did attract them, with his charm – were waiting to help him set up, as the van sagged and huffed to a halt. Swung open, the back doors revealed a piled assortment of blocks, cubes, cases, reels and a soft heap of material for use as blackout. The biggest pieces of equipment were the two loudspeakers, one grey, one dark brown, bulky wooden cubes so cumbersome and large that you felt they might actually store all the words and music required. On each, the top half of the front had curved protrusions for the sound to blossom from. A long, flattish case held two turntables on which, when he was showing silent films, Stuart played inventive combinations of music to accompany the action. It could be anything from Saint-Saëns's 'The Swan' to Barber's 'Adagio for Strings' to cascades of Liszt. The emphasis was often on pathos – music to die to rather than for. For Chaplin, energetic arpeggios for standing up to the bullyboy or the cop. For Keaton, riffs to make you smile while he didn't.

After the speakers, the next heaviest items to lug in were the two 16mm projectors, with their mottled brown casing and the precious eye of the lens embedded there, with its rainbow reflections. And wedged between everything else in the van were yards of electric cable, soft and black as liquorice, wound round fraying cardboard reels.

That left a screen to slide out from one of the torpedo tubes on the roof. Close to, it looked as if it had a coating of old emulsion paint which would soon crack and peel. There were side-pieces to fit into slots at the top and bottom, to stretch the yellowish-white surface. Then it had to be hoisted, wobbling and unsteady, to rest on chairs, or against a wall or a stage arch.

Sometimes we were allowed to sit by the entrance and take people's money. Like the unloading and setting up, this instilled in us a proud sense of importance. Stuart always gave us some silver to start off with: 'a float', he called it. At the end of the evening, we would count the takings and tell Stuart how much there was. 'Ah,' he would say, smiling his smile and sweeping the money off the table into his pocket.

Another essential preparation, almost a superstition, was anxiety about the size of the audience, especially if the weather was fine. 'I don't know if they'll come tonight,' Stuart would murmur, standing at the threshold. At schools, of course, there was never any difficulty, and even in out of the way villages the shows were generally well attended. Once people began to arrive, it got quite exciting, but just when the music had stopped and most of the lights been turned off, and you expected the film to start, Stuart would stride to the front and stand right in front of the screen, a silk handkerchief frothing impressively from the breast pocket of his jacket. Quietly he cleared his throat, an invitation to the audience to stop chatting; looked down at the ground, then up, smiling. 'Ladies and gentlemen, good evening.' If the talking didn't stop, as was frequently the case, the greeting was repeated, with a gulp of a chuckle and a glance across to the possible source of the noise. They might be impatient, but Stuart would doggedly have his say about the film to be shown, making mention of noteworthy techniques, the stars, the novelty of the film or its place in cinema history. It could seem to go on.

At last it began: the magic of sitting in the dark, listening to the ticking of the projector until soon you were captivated by the images twisting down the bluish beam of light. Towards the end of each reel, the ticking became more of a clacking, then came the instant at which the second projector took over, with a wobble and a momentary blur till the focus was adjusted. With silent films, there was the added pleasure of watching Stuart as he bent over the turntables where the 78s sped round, mixing the music by the light from a bulb crowned with a small tin as a shade. His eyes twinkled in the dimness, and his longish straight nose seemed almost to touch the surface of the record as he bent to find just the groove he wanted.

Going to schools with Stuart was different, but also good. They were boarding schools, nearly always, and more often than not girls' schools. We might have been creatures from a different planet. This was really good: the way the children looked at us, they with their uniforms and rules, we wearing what we wanted and free to come and go. But there was something forbidding about the atmosphere in such places – the long corridors reeking of polish, the sheaves of notices on boards, the distant coughing of cisterns. Stuart seemed to love it, and would be at his most urbane and charming as we sat sipping tea with the headmistress in her study. At his most mischievous too, pronouncing 'girls' as 'gels' and waggling his eyebrows, or breaking into a low Groucho Marx lope in the corridor and moving at speed.

There was plenty of time for talking, as we thundered along the roads of England. It was nearly always about films he had shown, or the one he was going to show. Virtually all his stories came from films with, by way of occasional variation, an anecdote told in a broad Devon accent, the upshot of his admiration for the stories of A. J. Coles, who wrote under the name of Jan Stewer. But I can't remember many occasions involving Stuart which were not directly to do with films. Even when we drove all the way to Brighton one penumbral November day, and squatted in the back of the steamed-up van with the primus hissing inside and the rain outside, it was to meet two Americans, George and John, who were allegedly in possession of a rare complete copy of Chaplin's *The Circus*, which they had smuggled into the country in 'the coffin', as Stuart remembered them calling their case.

In time I realised how complete his identification with the world of film was. It was as if he could himself be a man in a log cabin, at the edge of an abyss, fastidiously eating a Thanksgiving meal of boots, or a man in a darkened post-war city, in a doorway, with a cat running over his shoes. His was the hand which unnailed itself from the cross and reached down to accept a small boy's offering; his, the inner tube covered with fallen leaves and mistaken for a funeral wreath. His abraded sports jacket was in fact the duffel coat worn by Jack Hawkins looking out over the waves from the bridge. It was he who stood, scratching his head, while in front of him a piano cascaded, jangling, down a long flight of steps. The grey van might be a truck loaded with unstable nitroglycerine; or a horse-drawn caravan with, next to him, a strange sad girl half in love with a tightrope walker.

My parents' divorce went through in May 1946. Given that Amata was born a month later, I think it must have been before then that we went to stay with Daddy and Dolores in Brighton, where they were living. It is somehow astonishing to think that this might well have been, as I think it was, the last time that Trinny and I together stayed with Daddy on his own ground.

It cannot have been the easiest of occasions for anybody. Dolores was very kind and considerate to us. I remember Trinny and me being on the beach, by an upturned boat. There is a snapshot of us there, wearing dark overcoats and gloves. We slept in separate rooms. I was on a narrow divan alongside a large weaver's loom, a complicated-looking machine which Daddy tried to explain to me. I wetted the bed and was very upset.

We were in the sitting-room of the flat one day when Daddy came in upside down, walking on his hands. He had no shoes on, his feet were waving in the air, his trousers were falling up his legs. And how white they were, those legs, madly white! He came towards us unsteadily, paused to keep his balance, came on. Things started falling out of his trouser pockets: coins, a lighter, a comb. It was funny and grotesque. His face was going red, so was the top of his head. It was like the book with faces which we had at home: you could look at them either the right way up or upside down and they still made sense as faces, only the mouth became the eyebrows, the eyes became the nostrils, a beard became hair, and the chin, a bald forehead.

But was it our father, whichever way up? Because the other startling event of that visit was that he had become Gustav, a name we had never heard before. With Mummy he had always been Hellmut, which turned out to be his second name; with his second wife, it would always be his first that was used.

After Marian's death I explored the sheds 'down under'. In one, which had a ledge at waist height that ran a long way back, it was a matter of crawling into the dark with a torch. There seemed to be endless box files, some filled with newspaper cuttings, and hundreds of round cardboard containers with metal bases and lids. They were intended, presumably, for some future product. I also retrieved a favourite toy that had mysteriously gone missing some time before – a little metal speedboat which ran on solid white cubes of, possibly, methylated spirit, and spat water pleasingly from its twin exhaust pipes. The flame on the cube was as uncertain and ethereal as the little gulp of blue fire on a Christmas pudding.

I took a screwdriver to the small padlock on the door of the shed he had used as a laboratory. The interior was heavily cobwebbed, and not much light came through the single dusty window. There were rows of test-tubes with red or orange rubber corks, in wooden racks. Some had developed a lurid green growth inside: one had a pale blue liquid in it. My ignorance of science was complete, and Norwood certainly didn't offer anything in that line. I was once given a chemistry set, but was as apprehensive about using it as I felt now, looking round.

There was a musty, damp smell. A white mould was starting to form on the workbench, where a pipette lay beside a Bunsen burner. Water dripped intermittently from the tap of a Belfast sink in the corner. There was no sign of the cat

Charcoal – which, I realised only now, had not been in evidence for some time.

I wanted something momentous to be there, something which I could seize upon as a souvenir or, more exactly, a marker, a proof that this was territory that could be reclaimed. As it was, I went out empty-handed and dropped the latch. The place stayed like that, accumulating more dust and cobwebs than Miss Haversham ever dreamt of, till the day years later when we moved out.

*

Close to Fingle Bridge, a well-known beauty spot on the Teign, my mother bought a small square of land on a hillside dense with gorse and fern. She had the ground cleared and fenced and, with the help of Ernest Annerley (who had gone back to hairdressing) and the more reluctant assistance of Trinny and me, planted a young oak tree in Marian's memory. A small plaque at its foot included a quotation from Psalm 1: 'He shall be like a tree planted by the waterside, that will bring forth his fruit in due season'.

It could be said that all memorials become, in due season, tributes to amnesia. But in this instance, not quite. The oak has long since withered, and the concrete fence-posts fallen, but some perspicacious National Trust official, perhaps fearful of litigation or unsure what to do, has caused the plaque to be cemented into a low stone wall nearby.

*

A new teacher arrived at Norwood, a man quite tense in his manner, with a muscle in his cheek which twitched. He was an extremely sociable man, given to whist drives and bridge, and not so much a pillar of his local church as a vital part of its underpinning.

At school he was popular from the outset: when he was on playground duty, there was always a cluster of boys around him. He understood the ways in which their minds worked. He knew how to challenge and tease them, as well as how to flatter them. Often he would begin a conversation by saying something that seemed baffling or comic or plainly impossible, but there would always be some point to it, as finally became clear. This was a rather effective teaching method.

He cackled more than laughed, and when he was really amused his shoulders would shake. He could redeem himself from arrogance by turning his humour against himself. Above all, he seemed entirely at home in the undergrowth of school life, with its succession of conflicts and crazes, from vinegar-hardened conkers to water-pistols bright and transparent as wine-gums, most of them stolen from Woolworths.

The range of his knowledge seemed astonishing. He could tell you what a scrimshaw was, or how the plumage of young owls differed from the adults, or when the first transatlantic telephone cable was laid. The only perceptible gap was music, about which he knew very little, cheerfully declaring himself tone-deaf. He was extraordinarily organised, as suggested by his neat, clear handwriting. All appointments and invitations were noted in a small dairy. He also had a convertible car, which added greatly to his cachet.

I moved up into a class which he taught. Prep was always returned promptly, marked with a red fountain pen and with a score at the end. Full marks were never given. To my disappointment there were nearly always others who did better than me, though my marks were by no means a disgrace. He made you want to be top.

Gradually he got to know us at home, too. He took to calling in for a cup of coffee on his way to school in the morning. Sometimes he brought a jar of honey or some flowers or half a dozen eggs.

In our dining-room he sat relaxedly, giving out a small cloud of blue pipe-smoke, in the chair that Wolfy had occupied.

A summer evening in June 1954. Trinny, Mummy and I are in the office playing ping-pong – the mad version of it called 'progressive', with all three of us rushing round the table, hitting the ball in turn and trying to keep it in play. Suddenly the phone sounds shrilly from the corner. This seems astonishing, even though it must always ring here: usually we are down in the dining-room, and answer it there.

My mother picks up the receiver. Trinny and I go on playing half-heartedly, trying not to make too much noise. My mother doesn't speak much, and we don't pay much attention.

The next moment she has replaced the receiver and is in floods of tears. We have never seen her in quite this state before, not even when things have gone badly wrong. She looks very pale. We go over and put our arms round her, trying to comfort her. She is inconsolable. We have no idea what to do.

Finally, gulping and sobbing, she is able to tell us. Her father has died. We still don't know what to do.

*

It was about to happen. After all the imports from Austria, we were at last going to export ourselves there. For Trinny and me it was our first trip abroad, and it would have been some-how unthinkable to go to any other destination. The venture was given added glamour in our eyes when Mummy informed us that we were wards of court, and to leave the country we would therefore need the permission of the court as well as Daddy's agreement. To be a ward of court must, I thought, be a better condition than the fishy one suggested by the description of my mother, in a legal document which she had left lying around, as a 'femme sole'.

Mummy booked with a company called Tyrolean Travel, whose emblem was a double T made to look like a weather-house with fretted eaves and, in front of it, a man in *Lederhosen* wearing a pointed hat with a feather, and a woman in a *Dirndl*. The company took care of all the travel arrangements and accommodation, and there was a whole range of additional outings and excursions which we could undertake if we liked.

It was hard to see how the destination could possibly live up to the excitement of the journey there, particularly the overnight train. We had couchettes, but hardly slept and didn't want to. It was stifling. There were endless mysterious stops and starts. More than once the train, after stopping, set off in the opposite direction to the one in which it had been travelling before. And there was complicated clattering over points, junctions and crossings, to rhythms different from those of English trains.

About one o'clock in the morning we drew into the station at Basle: the platforms were deserted, apart from a man push-ing along a trolley loaded with snacks and hot sausages. When we got into the mountains the purplish-blue nightlight in the compartment was soon outdone by great forks of crackling lightning which we lifted the blind to see better. Further on, we halted for so long just beyond a station that I thought there might be no going on, for whatever reason. I got down from my couchette and peered out. This time there really was no one at all to be seen: just white lights staring down from immensely tall stems onto row after row of trucks in sidings. Then, fitful sleep after all – and waking in a dull glare of morning light to find the train rushing along beside a fierce grey-green river strewn with white boulders.

*

Schönruh, a small hotel looking down on Innsbruck from a hamlet called Aldrans, on the way up to the ski resort of Igls, could not have been better. Herr Jakob Tomasi and his family, who owned it, were very friendly, and my mother, who spoke fluent if not grammatical German, soon made friends with them. Trinny and I followed her example, getting to know Gerda, the daughter of the family. Her tan was emphasised by the red dress she often wore, and by her gleaming teeth. With her we had the kind of uncomplicated holiday friendship which makes a common language inessential. In any case, her English enabled a reasonable degree of communication, whereas our few words and phrases of German certainly didn't.

Between Innsbruck and Igls ran a tram route – small red and yellow cars with open balconies at either end, which wound their way up through the woods. There was a stop among the trees quite close to the hotel. The postbus, pale yellow with a black horn painted on its side, also went to and fro along a road with as many hairpin bends as if it had been toothpaste squirted from its tube. Its loud three-tone horn, used freely at most of the bends, marked its progress.

Mummy lost no time in furthering the process of assimilation. On our very first afternoon she took us down to the town to shop, returning with a *Dirndl* for Trinny and *Lederhosen* for me. All we needed was a weather-house, to be the complete incarnation of the Tyrolean Travel badge. For herself, she made do with a white Austrian cardigan which I think she already had, with silver buttons and embroidered with alpine flowers. She would always spend money on us before herself, much to the fury of Aunty Peggy, who despaired over Mummy's lack of interest in new clothes.

That night, under the strange bedcovers puffed-up like a giant pillow, we lay listening to the rain which suddenly was pelting down outside. The next morning, breakfast consisted of *Semmeln*, which were delicious crisp rolls, coffee and *Himbeersaft*, the raspberry's answer to Ribena, and better. Then it was our first journey on the tram – an outsize toy that snaked down its narrow track and, as you stood on the balcony, allowed you to see a little way into the dark heart of the forest.

It was to be our first meeting with Hans Zingerle. We knew that he had taught Mummy the piano when she was young; and that he had been a prisoner of war in Russia. Apparently he never spoke of this. We had also been told about the family castle in Italy, in the area which had formerly belonged to Austria.

Hans had a longish face with a kindly expression and, when he spoke, a nice way of pursing his lips slightly, especially when he was exercising his rather halting English. He was working on the music of William Byrd, whose name caused him particular difficulty, uncertain as he was about the pronunciation of that 'y'. 'Beerd', 'Baird', 'Burd', he would experiment smilingly, testing the possible vocalic variations and making us laugh. He had large hands, and ears which were quite large too, we noticed, but didn't stick out too much. That morning he took us all to a museum where there were, among other things, tableaux of waxwork peasants in parlours with tiled stoves. For us children, this visit was well on the moderate side of thrilling.

In the afternoon we had our first swimming lesson at a lovely open-air pool a short walk from the hotel. The *Schwimmeister*, broadly built, with racily slicked-back hair, dark glasses, and even more tanned than Gerda, struggled manfully to help us. By today's standards we were late starters, and neither of us was a natural swimmer. Trinny was, I thought, rather better at it than me. I found it very hard to keep the lower half of me anywhere near the surface. I'm not sure that either of us would have learnt but for the persistence of the *Schwimmeister*, who may have looked on us as a challenge.The attention of the many large horseflies round the pool certainly helped too: jerking convulsively when they bit us produced a movement not unlike a clumsy breast-stroke. Mummy was delighted when, after a week, she was able to record that we could manage up to eight strokes.

A daily pattern developed. Swimming for us, or playing table tennis with Gerda, while Mummy went into town to meet Hans. On several occasions we were allowed to spend the evening on our own at the hotel, which we thought very grown-up, while she and Hans had dinner. One night they went for a moonlit walk together. Did either of them recall that playing of 'Clair de Lune' on Hans's birthday seventeen years before? It was hard to know who was being the more grown-up, really, or in what way, and in any case our interests lay elsewhere.

Then there were the excursions with the others in the Tyrolean Travel group. Trinny and I thought that easily the best was to Neuschwanstein, the Disney-like castle built by King Ludwig II of Bavaria, with its fantastic turrets and improbable lavish interiors. And the story of how the king, said to be mad, drowned with his doctor in the lake you could see from the castle added greatly to the interest. For eleven-year-olds, the tour of the wardrobe department of the passion play theatre at Oberammergau or, for that matter, the brief visit on the way back to Mittenwald, with its violin-making tradition, hardly had the same appeal.

On one of the outings we had our first ride in a cablecar. It was a bit like a fairground ride in slow motion, with more slack and dip between the supporting pylons than you might have expected – or wanted. Easily the best moments, though also the most unnerving, were when the car passed over the pylons themselves, which made it dive forward, tip slightly, hesitate, rock backwards and then lurch forward again towards the next oncoming dip. As you got near to the top, the closeness of the mountain face outside was another cause of excitement compounded by fear.

One evening there was a display of Tyrolean dancing at the hotel, with much slapping of *Lederhosen* and shoe leather, not to mention dances with axe handles, and the occasional out-break of animal noises or yodelling. Every so often a cowbell or two was shaken. What struck me most of all was how out-size the dancers seemed, especially the men. This couldn't just be a local phenomenon, as the same had been true of a group of Morris dancers we saw at a fête at home. Perhaps it was what happened, in some odd way, when you dressed up to dance.

In the middle of our stay we went off to spend two days with the Zingerle family at the castle near Bolzano. We actu-ally stayed at the Gasthof Unterwirt, run by Herr and Frau Haselwanter, who remembered Mummy's and Daddy's pre-war visit, and were delighted to see her again and meet us. Schloss Summersberg was the kind of place a child might choose for paradise. It had everything – crenellated ramparts, a hall with a standing suit of armour, a chapel where the painted plaster figures induced just the right amount of shiver, a tower called The Witch's Tower, with a dungeon at its foot and a wooden staircase running up outside it to the top room, secret corners, terraces with a terrific view up over alms and pastures to the pale grey peaks and needles of the Dolomites, and lavatories which were just raised wooden seats at the top of a chute going down a long way to somewhere outside the castle walls. You could peer down and see a sunlit circle below, and rocks. It was tempting to sit there for longer than necessary, in the hot resinous gloaming.

This was to be the first of many visits, and we loved it. The castle was full of life, with the whole family there – Hans's brothers Berthold and Christoph, with their wives and children, and old Frau Zingerle, their mother, who presided with simple dignity and invited us to take acorn coffee with her in the castle's most formal room.

All too soon it was time to head back to Innsbruck and, shortly after, to return to England. If Mummy had felt any urge to justify her affection for Austria to us, she no longer needed to do so. We were sold on it, and swore to return the next year. Meanwhile we went home with an assortment of trophies: not only a generous supply of *Manners Neapolitaner*, but three wooden napkin rings, each decorated with a single flower – an edelweiss, a gentian and an alpine rose; and three small cowbells, one of which was to be used as a summons to meals. Once home, I lost no time in ruining several carriages belonging to my clockwork railway by taking the wheels off and attempting to convert them to cablecars.

Shortly after our return Trinny and I were outside in the

road, near to the land opposite Number 24, which was now having houses built on it. I was wearing my *Lederhosen*, which must have looked very out of place in Devon. More than that: the workers on the building site shouted and swore at me. What we children unselfconsciously associated with paradise could be someone else's reminder of hell.

Over the years the sea had been quietly infiltrating my soul. It is hard to know just when this began. Perhaps it was a simple consequence of being an islander, or that a love of the sea was always imprinted in the genes. There was, after all, my great-uncle Harold's *Cockbird*, the dinghy he kept at Sidmouth; and, more immediately, the presence of the sea in Daddy's pictures – astern of those beached boats, or girdling islands sometimes so vaguely drawn that they might have been drifting cloud.

I could pick out, in retrospect, any number of indirect seamarks, from the owl and the pussycat sailing away, to the exultant cry of Xenophon's men when at last they reached the coast. At school, the sea was well represented in prayers, hymns and poems – the ringing intercession for 'they that go down to the sea in ships, and occupy their business in great waters'; the eternal father whose arm binds the restless wave; Tennyson's crossing of the bar; Masefield's dirty British coaster.

Then there were many films in which the sea, cruel or not, played a central part. Films in which the likes of Kenneth More and Dirk Bogarde, draped with mighty binoculars over white polo-neck sweaters, anxiously scanned the horizon for U-boats, or skulked in their submerged submarine, periscope down, bracing themselves for the depth charges about to be unleashed by the enemy overhead. And pirate films like *The Crimson Pirate*, which had Burt Lancaster leaping tirelessly, sword in hand, from ratlines to gundeck. And of course the Pathé News, with its regular items about our naval prowess and maritime feats.

Books, too, played their part. The very first one to make a lasting impression arrived, as the inscription tells me, two months after my third birthday, a Christmas present from Uncle Basil. A large hardback book – to a three-year-old very large, its fourteen inches high by almost ten wide enough to give it immediate status: a book to wield as well as to read. The striking cover, in acidic lemon yellow, had the single word *Cocolo* in brown, in a bold freehand. Below this was a small outline sketch of a pot-bellied donkey with ears protruding from a wide-brimmed straw hat.

The first page is largely taken up by a picture of dolphins and large fish astern of a steamer making off. A cloud of smoke billowing from its funnel repeats the book's title, along with the author's name, given simply as 'Bettina'. Behind the fish, in the middle of a calm blue sea, lies a miniature sandy island, Ravaya-Reena, whose sole inhabitants turn out to be a fisherman, Babbo, his wife Mamma, their son Lucio and Cocolo the donkey.

A closer view of the island shows a simple white house, with a washing-line and a few vines alongside, a stand of tall pine trees, and a well at which Cocolo works, turning an overhead wheel to draw water. 'Sometimes he stopped to think. Then Lucio called out to him: "Go on Cocolo! Turn round Cocolo!" And Cocolo turned round and round and round.' This particular sentence is inseparable now from the memory of my mother's voice, her delight in reading it aloud.

The narrative is triggered by an unintended visit to the island by one Mr Fatimus Greedy and his daughter Fussy. A trip in their smart motor-boat goes horribly wrong when Mr Greedy carelessly shifts his bulk, causing the boat to capsize.

111

Babbo rescues them. The next morning, 'when Fussy saw Cocolo in the sunshine, she loved him so much that she said she would not leave Ravaya-Reena unless he came with her'. Seduced by the prospect of enough money to buy new nets, Babbo agrees to sell Cocolo.

In his new home Cocolo becomes as spoilt as Fussy herself, then homesick. Trying to find his way home, he falls into the hands of Professor Fame, owner of a piano on wheels who busks to finance his drinking. Then by chance Lucio, bringing fish caught with the new strong nets to sell, spots Cocolo and takes him back to the palatial Greedy residence. They all go back to Ravaya-Reena, where Cocolo turns the wheel of the well again and there is much merrymaking. The final picture shows the townees heading back, after dark. By the pine trees, under a sky peppered with stars, Lucio and Cocolo 'stood watching the boat until they could hear and see it no longer'.

The world *Cocolo* evokes is the hot south, the Mediterranean at its most alluring, with more than a hint of Italy in the appearance of the Greedy palazzo, the town streets and a road with sentinel cypresses that winds along by the sea. As for the island, it is Arcadia writ small, a simple enclave from which a child reader might conjure an Edenic idyll.

I learned later that Bettina was the writing name of Bettina Bauer, born in Vienna in 1903. In 1930 she married the sculptor Georg Ehrlich. They were forced to emigrate, and came to London in 1938 – four years after my father had done likewise.

*

Then came *Treasure Island*, *The Coasts of Barbary*, Captain Hornblower and heaven knows how many other swashbuckling tales. Not to mention the adventures of Storm Nelson in the *Eagle*.

*

The nearest sea to home lay tantalisingly close, only ten miles away at Exmouth. The river Exe ran down to it like a gleaming umbilical. And though being on the beach, or even doing the trip round the bay, was good enough for a time, in the end it left me sulky and frustrated. Appalling displays of petulance, no doubt, and the scuffing of shoes on deliberately kicked quayside furniture.

It was our dentist, Mr Rainey, who offered a solution, thus earning instant promotion from the lowly position he and his grinding drill held in my mind. He knew of a sailing club in Salcombe, the Island Cruising Club, which ran courses for beginners. Mummy wrote to find out how much it would cost, and I made a solemn promise to myself to be better about cleaning my teeth.

*

A launch with a stubby mast flying the club's green pennant collected me and my fellow beginners from the customs house quay and headed up towards The Bag, the broadest part of the estuary – or, to be accurate, the drowned river. We were soon at the ex-motor torpedo boat moored to one side of the main channel, which was to be our base. We were deposited at a pontoon alongside, where the boats in which we would learn were also moored.

It was quite a strict régime, with potato peeling and deck scrubbing and, on most days, instruction about everything from the principles of sailing to knots and splices to be got through before we were allowed to take to the boats. There was naming of parts, too: tacks and clews, sheets, figures of eight, rolling hitches and all the rest.

We learnt in fourteen-footers, clinker built and gaff rigged, with dark red sails. For the moment we remained in or close to The Bag and the harbour. Later, we would be allowed to venture seaward towards the Wolf Rock then, later still, over the bar and into the first heave of the swell. On the way we would leave North Sands to starboard, with Hazeldene School somewhere in the trees above and behind the beach. It was strange to think that Salcombe, which neither Trinny nor I had heard of not so long ago, now engaged with both of our lives.

Upstream lay a different kind of challenge, the narrowing channel which wound its way between mudbanks up to Kingsbridge. It was only really navigable on a good spring tide: and it was considered an achievement to get to the top of the estuary with sufficient time for a cream tea, before heading back.

This was total immersion, so to speak – to live on the water day and night, to be aware of the sea's great muscle turning languidly or with a twitch underfoot, to hear the wind thrum in the halyards, to lick the tangy salt from your lips. Above all, to listen to the chuckle of the water under the hull as the dinghy made way; to brace yourself as the wind caught the sails and the boat heeled over, dipping the lee gunwale into the foam. And once, after dark, I was allowed to row a tiny snub-nosed pram round the headland towards the town. Small lights everywhere, in the cabins of anchored boats, at the mastheads of a few under way, along the harbour front and across the town, reaching up the hill behind it: and a great star-pricked darkness presiding. From my little boat shallow as a saucer, whirlpools of phosphorescence twisted away and down at each pull on the oars. The night breeze was cool on my cheek. I knew then how Trinny had felt when one night, looking out over Innsbruck from the hotel, she had suddenly burst into tears. 'It's all too beautiful,' she had said.

This love of the sea has stayed with me, and I return to it again and again. Protean, never the same twice, even when you look quickly away and back, the sea's shifting totality is virtually beyond verbal encompassing, unless you have the inclusive exuberance of Whitman or Walcott, or the linguistic dazzle of Rimbaud or Bunting. The sea's teeming narratives have no end. Advance, retreat, overfalls, cross-currents, undertow, swash: the sea rampant and inroading, the sea grey and crouched low. The sea thunderous and roaring, or silent and sunlit in dazzling skeins. The oddity of rain at sea, water pooling on water, and the novelty of the land seen from the ocean's plunging deck.

Two other memories stay from my first days of sailing at Salcombe. Firstly, the intense and changing colour of the water, which could be ultramarine one day, a brilliant green on its way to being emerald the next, an opaque grey-blue after that. And then, in The Bag, there was an oak wood which ran right down to the water's edge, where salt had trimmed the lowest branches level, leaving a fine secret zone of dark shade beneath the overhang. In that shadow was where I wanted to be.

I only remember Daddy coming to stay once at Union Road, though there were day visits on other occasions. By then he had for some time lived in Burton-on-Trent, where he had worked at the School of Art and Crafts since 1949. Burton, Bromborough, Brighton – was he in some mysterious way in hock to the second letter of the alphabet? If so, why had 'Barbara' not worked?

Each time you saw him, it was the beauty of his light blue eyes which you had never quite remembered properly from the last time. On arriving, he bent down to kiss us first on one cheek and then on the other. This brought with it a distinctive whiff, a mixture of cigar and shaving soap. He would press his face quite firmly against yours, so that at the instant of the kiss you were mildly stung by his stubble, a prickling sensation which was more than a rough towel and less than insect bites. It tingled a bit.

He brought Amata with him: I don't think we had met her before. Our poor half-sister: here she was in a strange place, suddenly confronted with two other children who had claims on her father's attention and affections. As an only child, she must have found it hard to cope with. Trinny and I felt rather as we had when Marian's relatives came to see us: somewhat baffled and unsure what to do. Amata spoke and laughed loudly, obviously ill at ease, and made a point of sitting on Daddy's lap and wrapping her arms round him. She looked at us as if daring us to do something about it.

It may have been during this visit that Daddy took me aside and produced an object smooth as a skimming-stone, and as tightly closed as a bivalve's shell. It was a flat, slender pocket watch with a case of silver, though more the duller colour of gun-metal. Its hands were needle thin, except where there was a slight bulbous extension on the hour hand, just before it came to a point. An inner circle of black numbers had the 5 and the 7 interrupted by a small dial with an even finer and smaller hand showing the seconds. Round the periphery of the face ran an outer circle of numbers in red, from 13 to 24. The winder protruding at the top was surrounded by a thin silver ring to which a watch chain could be attached, but wasn't. The back of the watch was decorated with three circles engraved close to the edge, one inside another, and crossed with an 'x' twelve times just where the hours would be marked.

I had already come to hallow some of the objects in the house which I could associate with Mummy's and Daddy's life together, such as the great stainless steel saucepan, made in Finland, with the number of litres it could hold in small italic numerals near the rim: 3,5 with a comma rather than a decimal point. They had bought it in Tottenham Court Road. Or the Quimper jug, cracked and with its handle glued back into place, decorated with a man wearing a round hat and carrying a walking stick.

This was in a different league altogether. Daddy explained that the watch was handed down to the eldest son in each generation, and he wanted me to have it now. I was quite overwhelmed. Everything about the watch was perfect: the slimness and elegance of it, the red numerals marching along outside the black ones, the conspiratorial quietness of its ticking when I held it to my ear.

After Daddy and Amata had gone back to Staffordshire, I sat on my bed and prised the hinged back of the watch open. On the inside of the cover, and visible only when angled to the light, someone had written a name and a date. Puzzlingly, the name wasn't our own. When I asked Mummy about this, she laughed. 'Didn't I tell you?' she said lightly.

It transpired that her mother had not just been opposed to the marriage because her daughter was marrying an artist, though that was bad enough. But to marry a German as well! Apparently she had said as much to his face and suggested that he change his name. 'Why not, for instance, Sail? After all, you love the sea, don't you?' Astonishing that she should have gone so far as to dream up a name, and even more, given his natural obstinacy and independence, that my father had gone along with this. Further evidence, if any were needed, of the hold love can exert over reason.

I was torn between enjoyment of this secret and something more unsettling. What would it be like if I changed my own name back to a German one? Should I? Was it legal? How could I not? I thought of those swearing builders, then of the Germans in the comics – lantern-jawed, doltish, their helmets always looking half a size too big. All they ever seemed to say was *Achtung!* or *Donner und Blitzen!* or *Englischer Schweinhund!* apart from a screech-word – *Aaaargh!* (the equivalent of the *Aieeee!* emitted by Red Indians in westerns) as they somersaulted to their death, blown out of a pillbox, tank or trench by a well-aimed grenade lobbed by the brave Tommies.

I thought of the big *Times* atlas in the bookcase, in which during the war my father had overpainted in black all those countries that had fallen victim to the Third Reich.

And how could our mother not have told us before now?

Back in my room, I got my compass out of my satchel and with its point clumsily scratched *L. R. Sail* inside the back cover of the watch, close to *Schmitt*. In bed that night I tried out my German name on the darkness. *Schmitt, Schmitt. Messerschmitt. Schmittfire. Donner und Schmittzen!*

Memory, like the world of dreams, has its apparent inconsequences, some of them quite impenetrable. Why, for instance, should mine have preserved so minutely the basting spoon in the kitchen at Union Road – the handle at an obtuse angle to the bowl, the top of it pea-green plastic, and the bowl marked inside with rings giving the measure of set amounts? It has no associations, no iconic value, yet there it is, as securely lodged in the mind as it used to be in the long drawer of the kitchen table.

Other objects of recall are easier to fathom, such as my mother's light brown handbag which included, among other things, a pale pigskin wallet lined with shot silk, her powder compact, a small bottle of the Worth perfume 'Je reviens' which was the only scent she used, and a lump or two of sugar with which she would console us in the event of a mishap. When once I swayed backwards from a low wall into a boating pool, as a result of laughing too much at something in a Punch and Judy show, it was one of her lumps of sugar which stopped me howling.

But as with the basting spoon, there are some incidents from early childhood which remain mysteriously present and immediate, their very persistence giving them a status they might not deserve.

*

I have spent much of the morning in church, sitting next to a school friend whose father is a priest. I haven't been here

120

before. The church, built recently, is filled with people, all of whom appear to know what they are doing. There are lots of flowers, but not enough to account for the slightly sickly smell of the place.

The service starts with a long procession headed by a man in a white robe. He is swinging a small gold bucket on the end of a long gold chain. Every so often he hauls in the chain and waves the bucket in the direction of the congregation. It clanks loudly and a cloud of sweet-smelling smoke puffs out, like a minor version of the steam shooting up from the train as it goes under the bridge near the football ground.

There is an awful lot of chanting. Several times there is the sound of an unseen tinkly bell. People keep on getting up or kneeling, or touching their forehead and chest and shoulders with one hand. I feel desperately ill at ease.

Now a man is climbing up into the pulpit to talk to us. His throat is bandaged with a white scarf, and he is wearing a funny little black hat which he takes off and parks on the rim of the pulpit. He begins. He goes on, with wide gestures now and then which make the kind of cloak he is wearing billow out.

Looking round, I see a crucifix. The figure on it leans forward, head bowed, arms stretched to the terrible fixing nails from which rivulets of blood run down. The head is blotched with blood, too, and topped with a prickly nest of thorns. Below the ribs, there is a bloody slot on one side, with drops of blood on the loincloth below. What could it be like to wear a loincloth, I wonder, and feel ashamed at the thought: as I do at the realisation that the flesh of Christ, its pale grey tint, reminds me of nothing so much as the hot kaolin poultices which Mummy applies if either of us is unfortunate enough to have a boil. Left to draw the poison, it is then removed, often with a disgusting though interesting mixture of pus and blood at its centre.

Blood – and smoke, a whole lot more of it pouring from the gold smoke-bucket. At the end of the service it hangs in the air in small pungent drifts. It stays in my nostrils like a sweetness put there to disguise something else. I think of the little bag filled with rustling lavender seeds which my mother puts into the drawer with my clothes.

*

I am alone in the drawing-room at Union Road. I have been looking at a book about the Ancient Egyptians, in whom I have developed a great interest. I am trying to understand what the author is explaining about hieroglyphics, and can't somehow take it in. I am sitting back on my haunches in front of the bookcase, close to the piano.

Without warning, like sudden intense heat from the door of a furnace swung open, it comes to me that words have an extraordinary power which I must somehow learn to commandeer. It almost knocks me sideways, just the excitement of it. And then comes a calm voice, speaking clearly inside my head. It says: you will have to live every day, every hour, every minute in this body of yours. Every breath in and out, till the end. Never a day off, as long as you are alive, never the chance to look at yourself from somewhere else.

These two quite different propositions run alongside one another in my mind. Parallel lines, I remember being told in school, never meet.

*

It is a warm afternoon. I am in the large garden attached to a friend's house. His parents have a dog which I distrust completely, though I usually like dogs. This one is a large animal with large teeth, and a short tail curled up over its back. It looks as if it would be happier tearing other animals to pieces than being taken for walks. It also knows instinctively that I am frightened of it and tenses, letting out a menacing low growl whenever I pass close to it, a situation that I do my best to avoid.

The garden is divided into two by a wall running between the formal lawn and a more informal area, which is where my friend and I happen to be. Suddenly there is a scream. We run over to the wall in time to see a woman being pursued by the dog. It gains on her; she turns to face it. It leaps at her and bites her nose, which starts to bleed profusely. Someone appears, carrying a large stick, and calls the beast off.

I can almost feel the way in which its teeth sink into the nostrils.

*

Mummy has allowed me to put up a small tent on the back lawn, in which a friend and I are to spend the night. It is made of waxed green canvas, rather heavy and with just about enough room for the two of us. When the time comes, we change into our pyjamas in the house and go out to bundle ourselves and our sleeping-bags into the tent.

It turns out to be a stifling summer night. We lie on our backs outside the bags, trying to get comfortable, to get cool. It still isn't properly dark outside. There is a slight peppery sweetness in the motionless air.

'Are you asleep?'

'No. Are you?'

Ha ha. Why are we whispering? We keep turning over, or

propping ourselves up on an elbow to see if the other has in fact fallen asleep.

Finally I doze off – but only to wake again (after how long?). It is completely dark now, but hotter than ever, because I am being held in a hug. There is a tummy pressed against mine. It is sticking out a bit, and I can feel his pyjama cord against my skin. This is strange enough, but even stranger is that my friend isn't saying anything at all, just clutching at me a bit in a kind of embrace. Are his eyes open or is he asleep? Now he's making a low murmuring noise. I decide that, despite the heat, the best thing is just to lie here. His skin smells of something.

I can feel the sweat running down past my ear and into the collar of my pyjama jacket. Am I awake or asleep myself? Why is he hugging me, and why don't I mind?

In the grey of morning we are lying apart, my friend hiding behind the wall of his back. When we get up, nothing particular is said. Mercifully, the temperature has dropped by a few degrees.

S tuart Keen asked Mummy to be secretary of the Exeter Film Society, which he ran in addition to all the juggling acts that made up his life. Like other societies of the same kind, it put on a wonderful range of films, many of them from abroad, and some either no longer widely obtainable or unlikely ever to get commercial distribution. Mummy's work, unpaid, would be principally to distribute agendas and take minutes at the meetings of the society's committee. She took it on gladly, as later she took on being secretary of the local Save the Children Fund committee.

She was good at this kind of thing, efficient and conscientious, and it prevented her from being lonely, as well as providing a riposte to the feeling of being useful to no one which sometimes took hold of her. She needn't have worried: she had a real gift for befriending and helping people. At the same time, committee work and the sort of temperament it suggests were quite alien to another side of her character, which went for spontaneity and improvisation.

She was, above everything else, an enthusiast, and did her best to graft her own interests onto her children. Thus Trinny and I were regularly taken up to the tennis courts at the top end of the road and coached by Mummy, who insisted that we throw the ball really high when serving, and hit it with a really straight elbow as it came down. She also organised piano lessons for us, as well as playing on her own account. She let us have the run of her considerable collection of gramophone records. She taught us to count in

German, and encouraged an interest in other countries too, especially France and Spain, both countries that she knew well from her travelling days. She loved speaking French as much as she did German.

As for learning to cook, we were allowed to bake cakes and pastries, taking over the kitchen on our own and turning out biscuits in particular in industrial quantities, cutting the pastry into rounds with a silver napkin ring. Mummy never blanched when faced with the sometimes severe test of responding with apparent delight to the results of our efforts. Once, after finishing up what was left of the seventy-two biscuits we had baked, like a priest consuming the left-over wafers at the end of communion, I threw up wholeheartedly into the hedge by the front gate. No one was to know apart from Trinny, who had witnessed the scene, but I felt very guilty and feared exposure when, a few days later, the leaves of the hedge turned from green to bright yellow. Mummy's own enjoyment of food was guaranteed for a time by Eva's stylish cooking. After she and Isolde had gone, it was more often a question of the few dishes which Mummy, with her dislike of cooking, was prepared to produce. Not that these were bad – main courses were either steak or stew; what followed, when it wasn't fruit, alternated between bread and butter pudding and a chocolate pudding made with cornflour, which came out as a cross between a mousse and an opaque blancmange.

In the post-Eva era Mummy would sometimes take us out to a meal, either at a restaurant serving rather fatty steak, which she always declared to be very good whatever it was actually like, or to the Clock Tower Café, where we always had roast lamb with the texture of an old school satchel. It was served with imploded roast potatoes and a mint sauce in which a few strands of the herb had been soused in strong malt vinegar.

We were too young to take much interest in cars, especially as Mummy didn't own one, but this didn't stop her regaling us with tales of early motoring: how it used to be the thing to clean the windscreen with a sliced potato or apple, or how it had sometimes been necessary to reverse up a hill, if the petrol tank were close to empty. And when we went to Austria, she bought us each a small clockwork car with a steering wheel which actually turned the wheels and a horn that croakily did its business when pressed.

For Mummy, books were always part of the equation. Once we had got beyond Beatrix Potter, Brer Rabbit, Winnie the Pooh and a series about a koala bear called Wonk, she would read her own favourites to us. Getting beyond Beatrix Potter wasn't quite as easy as it sounds. Even before my German was good enough to tell me just how sinister Mr Tod was by name as well as by nature, there seemed to be an undertow of darkness in many of the stories.

The top places in Mummy's pantheon were not in doubt: *Alice's Adventures in Wonderland*, *Through the Looking-glass*, *Gulliver's Travels, Peter Pan* and almost anything by Dickens. She had a particular liking for a short story of his called *The Magic Fishbone*, which I have never come across anywhere else, though I still have her now rather tatty copy.

Among the books which gave me greatest pleasure as a child, in addition to almost any seafaring yarns, were Anthony Buckeridge's stories about the schoolboy Jennings and his friend Darbishire, Richmal Crompton's *Just William* books, Saki's short stories and a series of thrillers by Malcolm Saville. The first of these I read, presented to me by Mummy, was *The Alpine Rose*. I'm sure she chose it for its title.

As well as the single books which she put our way, and frequent trips to the library to get more, there was Arthur Mee's *Children's Encyclopaedia*, all ten volumes of it. Each volume contained entries which went from stirring tales of heroic deeds to ways of improving your French (such handy demotic phrases as the French for 'the nursemaid helps the children to pack their toys'), to 'Things to Do on a Rainy Day' – cue the poor little things looking out from a boxroom across the gale-swept acres of the estate. One thing to do on a rainy day – and all the activities proposed under this heading were surely designed to keep the children's hands out of their pockets – was to learn 'how to knock a brick flat upon a table'.

What we didn't realise at the time was the rigorous system of morality which enclosed Mr Mee's world. British people were, on the whole, good and Christian and given to noble actions, witness David Livingstone, Jack Cornwell and Grace Darling. Foreigners were generally speaking inferior, though there were certain exemptions such as Joan of Arc, depicted in full armour looking heavenwards from the flames, with a caption beneath the picture reading 'The Stainless Maid of France', a bit confusingly since her armour looked to be made of steel.

Cavemen and others who couldn't be expected to know much about anything were 'jolly'. The same might have been true of the glistening Africans clad in the merest of loincloths, who stood in clearings in front of helmeted explorers in full fig. Loincloths were, of course, compulsory in these illustrations; by the same token Michelangelo's David, in common with all the other classical statues in the encyclopaedia, had been airbrushed to neuter, with nothing at all between his thighs.

'Good', 'bad' and 'jolly' were not, however, permissible terms for the perceived real baddies, that is to say 'negro bands', consumers of gin and Germans. A photograph of Arras town hall reduced to ruins during the First World War simply had underneath it 'The Mark of the Beast'. Mr Mee liked his capital letters.

Quite distinct from books was the pleasure to be had from comics. One of the great things about them was that grown-ups rarely wanted to share them, or read over your shoulder, or read them to you. You could keep them to yourself. The range of people and creatures you encountered was phenomenal, from Desperate Dan to Cardew Robinson, Billy Bunter to Lettice Leaf, Felix the Cat to Spiderman, and all the rest. There were also penny dreadfuls, those forerunners of the graphic novel. In some of them, in addition to the story there were enticing advertisements for crystal radio sets, and Charles Atlas smiling broadly as he flexed his astonishing musculature. But it was the *Eagle* I liked best, though it was a relative latecomer on the scene, and even though the biblical tale at the back of each issue was tiresomely pious in tone. What really appealed to me was Dan Dare, and in particular his sworn foe the Mekon, a bulbous-headed green midget with mean yellow eyes who rode the air on a kind of stream-lined gravy boat. But he was run a close second by tales in other comics, of the kind in which our hero, cornered by the villain, has been tied down beneath a small tank of concentrated sulphuric acid, which is creeping towards him on rails across the ceiling. How can he possibly escape?

*

Is parental love shared out equally? Perhaps so sometimes, and in any case parents themselves may need to believe that it is. Where there is only one parent for most of the time, such a belief is likely to become an imperative.

The trouble was that I showed a greater inclination to follow many of Mummy's interests than Trinny did. Given the limitations of Trinny's schooling, I had much more of an opportunity to do so. There was also the uncomfortable truth that from quite a young age I began to occupy at least some of the space left by Daddy's absence. I carved the meat, and ordered the meal or called for the bill in a restaurant. It was I who played piano duets with Mummy, not Trinny.

To some extent this had to do with the view of the sexes current at the time, and it was also a matter of differences of temperament and aptitudes between Trinny and me which were not to be blamed on anyone. But it had a doubly bad effect, making me in some ways horribly precocious and imposing on Trinny the same self-doubt and lack of confidence that Mummy had suffered at the hands of her own mother.

Mummy was half aware of this, and would say that unlike her mother she would never make a favourite of one child at the expense of the other, or be possessive. Unfortunately, articulating these shortcomings gave her a kind of alibi which then rendered her oblivious to the ways in which she might be repeating her mother's behaviour. For me, it made for difficulties later in trying to work free of home. I would be unkind, then feel guilty, then angry at being made to feel guilty, and the anger would make me be unkind again. Such things must have played a part, too, in the onset of the chronic depression which has come to determine too much of Trinny's life.

*

Nothing is more particular than a family, less open to generalisation. Yet it does seem that often, beyond conspicuous or dramatic events, almost too much becomes invisible in the relationship between parents and young children – either by being taken for granted, or simply forgotten. How could it ever be possible to recall exactly, let alone honour fully, all the minutiae of daily caring for their children which is the lot of parents? The sleep foregone, the washing, cleaning, consoling, cooking, the hunt for the vital missing toy, the salve for the grazed knee or the burning gums: all shake down to the abrasions of the everyday and are finally subsumed by time. Likewise, on the other side, the child's arm thrown about the parent's shoulder, the shrieks of a joy honed by apprehension as the children run to escape the monster, the look in the child's eye as its mother and father lean over in turn with a goodnight kiss, or the smell of safety in a mother's dress.

This is not a matter of sentimentality, but a groundswell too often flattened beneath the busyness of our lives and the onrush of time. To mention it is to express nothing more or less than the hope that our judgements of family life may be less coarse and sweeping, more mindful of the affectionate rhythms which underlie the everyday. Or, to come full circle, to hope for that in the particular case of my judgements, my parents.

The friendship which appeared to be developing with the teacher was strange but enjoyable. What made it strange was the mixture of hot and cold, his tendency to encourage me at times and to put me down at others, as it seemed to me. On some occasions I was made to feel important and successful, on others, I was apparently a disappointment. What made it enjoyable were the outings which began to happen – either in the company of another boy from school, or else on my own. Sometimes Mummy and Trinny would come along too, on an excursion in his car or to have tea at his house.

The car was wonderful, as probably any car would have been that wasn't one of Mr Peachey's lame steeds. To bowl along the lanes with the hood down in spring, when the hedgerows were bright with salads of pale tender primroses, or under beech trees sticky with buds against the intense blue of the sky, was almost as exhilarating as sailing, with the wind turning your hair to a mad wick and making conversation impossible.

There were picnics on Dartmoor, sumptuous lunches packed in a wicker hamper the teacher got out from the boot: rolls, Scotch eggs, pork pies at the very least. Sometimes there was a visit to a stone circle, where the teacher would point out the sites of huts and the wall which had once enclosed them. Sometimes we would climb to the top of a tor and look down towards the coast. Or we would sit by a stream, beneath a rowan tree foaming with creamy flowers or, later in the year, heavy with orange-red berries. It was not unheard of for him to throw out a general knowledge question now and then.

Wherever we went, the teacher took quite a lot of photos, using his hand to shade the cross-shaped viewfinder of his black camera. It had a lens that slid forward on runners when you opened the case.

As time went on, I was allowed to fill his pipe for him, and even, when we were on a deserted open road on the moor, to operate the gear lever.

*

The first visit to Austria had been such a success that Mummy was determined to go again the following year: this time for nearly three weeks, rather than under two.

On the way out we had a meal in London with my mother's cousin Pam and her parents, Paddie's sister Clare and her husband Dagnall, as we had on the way back the year before. Pam, a lively bird-like divorcée, was tremendous fun and Trinny and I loved her easily. Dagnall and Clare lived in Westminster, in a flat which had an Epstein bronze, 'Mother and Child', on a chest of drawers in the hall. The child's head was angled up from the base of the sculpture, close to the mother's hanging breast. We stared at it with a mixture of fascination and uncertainty. In the sitting-room a Marini horseman scanned the ceiling anxiously. Among the paintings on the walls, two were invisible under drapes. We were allowed to look at them. They were pale, washed-out watercolours, one of them of Venice, by someone called Turner, we were told, and had to be protected from the light lest they fade.

This time we were bound for Salzburg, again under the aegis of Tyrolean Travel. The holiday looked set to be a near repeat of the year before. Like all sequels, it risked inducing disappointment, not least because the weather was very variable, with frequent downpours and thunderstorms: and it was hard to see how it could recapture the thrill and intensity of being abroad for the very first time.

As at Innsbruck, we stayed in a village outside the town, at the Hotel Freisacher in Anif, and as before, there was a swimming pool on the edge of some woods. And again there were excursions, the best of them to a salt mine with an underground lake and a narrow railway better than any fairground ride. You sat astride a central bar and raced along at what seemed a fantastic speed through dripping, narrow tunnels. The most boring outing, from my point of view and Trinny's, was a tour of a factory making nylon stockings, though it caused Mummy to discourse about Palmers stockings and the difficulty of obtaining seamless nylons in the aftermath of the war. There was also a boat trip on the Wolfgangsee: Mummy got very excited at seeing the original setting for the operetta *The White Horse Inn*. Back in Salzburg, another operetta – *Die Fledermaus* at the puppet theatre. To us, this was considerably better than the event which Mummy considered the cultural highlight of our stay, a production of the Richard Strauss opera *Ariadne auf Naxos*, with Erich Kunz and Hilde Güden in the cast and Karl Böhm conducting. We knew that it was something we were meant to like and think important, but it was completely beyond us, and it didn't help that the packed auditorium of the *Festspielhaus* was incredibly hot. The evening seemed even longer than the last lesson at school before lunch, when you are almost giddy with hunger and can hardly keep your eyes open.

We were surprised to see American soldiers in Salzburg. It was easy to forget that the war had been over for barely ten years, and that the town was still in the American zone of occupation. Someone said drily that the Americans were to be seen everywhere, unlike the French troops in Innsbruck who came into town only to get more wine and new girlfriends. For the French, it was said, occupation was a personal matter and had more to do with the local talent than anything else.

There was shopping, too. Amazingly, Mummy spent some money on herself, buying a *Dirndl*, pink with a close pattern of small white flowers, and a blue apron. I was bought a pointed green hat with a feather, which I don't remember ever wearing, and a grey felt jacket with green lapels, a high collar and buttons pretending to be of wood. It was while we were in Salzburg that Trinny and I received a picture post-card each from England, sent by the teacher. Very kind of him, Mummy thought.

We had plenty to do and see in Salzburg, but it was with a pleasurable sense of homecoming that we went on to Innsbruck for the last week of our stay. I think we must have broken free of Tyrolean Travel, because we stayed in very simple bed and breakfast accommodation in the town: no running water, noted Mummy, though I find this hard to believe. No hot water, perhaps. We did have meal coupons issued by Tyrolean Travel, presumably as a way of supple-menting the quite meagre sums you were allowed to take abroad under the terms of the Exchange Control Act. However, Mummy soon noticed that when we produced the coupons in a restaurant, the main menu was at once replaced by a special one. Deducing that 'special' actually meant 'infe-rior', she determined to do without the coupons, at least for as long as our cash lasted.

Gerda had come to meet the train, and we were delighted to

see her: in fact we spent much of our time going up to Schönruh, not least to enjoy the tram ride to get there. The other focus of our stay was the Café Schindler, halfway along the town's main thoroughfare, the Mariatheresienstrasse, and close to a column surmounted by a statue of St Anne, her head permanently on the verge of being hoop-la'ed by a gold halo with stars round its rim. If Mummy had herself been an occupying force, the Café Schindler is where she would have made her headquarters. It was just the kind of place she loved: plush seats, papers in bamboo holders not unlike rectangular versions of carpet-beaters, a spectacular selection of cakes vying with one another in architectural complexity and rich fillings, and an enticing aroma of freshly ground coffee. Nothing made her happier than to sit gazing into a large cup in which a gradually dissolving berg of whipped cream rotated slowly, inhaling the fragrant fumes of the coffee beneath. 'Kaffee mit Schlag', she would murmur, to no one in particular.

Mummy's usual fiscal prudence seemed to have deserted her. Not only had she bought herself that *Dirndl* in Salzburg; now she decided to buy Hans a portable Olivetti type-writer for his birthday. But where was he? At the castle, presumably – where, much to our disappointment, we would not be going this time. He turned up halfway through our stay, and the same kind of routine emerged as in the previous year. The four of us would spend the day together, and in the evening Trinny and I would go up to Schönruh or back to our lodgings while Mummy went to Hans's rather sober flat. We went there too, during the day, and he played Debussy to us: we particularly liked 'The Golliwog's Cakewalk'. He also had long-playing records, and wanted us to listen to Carl Orff's *Carmina Burana*, with its mighty per-cussive opening and chorus: 'O fortuna'.

During this and subsequent visits we got to know Hans a bit better. He was considerate and thoughtful to us children, and we liked the way in which he treated us almost as grown-ups. He would buy us paperbacks about well-known artists, with coloured plates, which were really very good. And he would always try to include us in the conversation, despite his relative lack of English, and ours of German. He used three German phrases which he repeated often in his deep, resonant voice. One was directed at Mummy – 'Abfälle vom Tisch der reichen Frau' ('Crumbs from the rich woman's table'); one at Trinny and me, usually while we were looking at a view – 'Ist das nicht *schön*, Kinder?' ('Isn't that *beautiful*, children?'); and one to all three of us – 'Wir wollen also einen kleinen Ausflug machen' ('So let's go on a little excursion'). Of these phrases, the first was the hardest to fathom, even when translated.

As for the 'little excursion', we really found out what that meant two days before we were due to leave, when the four of us caught a train southwards to Matrei and went walking in the High Tauern mountains. It was the archetypal Austrian hill walk: up through maize glistening in the sun, past fields where the hay was stooked round a single vertical pole, just as in a Monet painting; into cool, resinous woods deep in shadow with, every so often, a wayside shrine or a wooden footbridge over a noisy, steeply falling stream; out onto a green alm, where pale brown cattle grazed languidly, occasionally clattering a bell; back into more woods; and finally out onto a high plateau where rock showed through the grass, and weathered peaks stretched away ahead. Here we spread out a picnic of speck, ham and cheese. Then, peaches almost as big as grapefruit, from which the sweet juice spurted out and ran up your arms. Afterwards we lay back, tired but contented, staring idly up at the sky.

On the way back we made a detour to go through a village. At someone's suggestion we looked into the church. Hans went into one of the pews and, in a way that was entirely natural but also devout, knelt to pray. Was he, I wondered with no good reason, thinking of his time of imprisonment in Russia?

*

Our second visit to Austria left me feeling rather disconcerted. For all the brightness of the place, the house walls with murals and the gaudy geraniums leaning out from the wooden balconies of chalets, there was an underlying feeling of menace which I could not define. It had something to do with death, which was not a subject I understood at all. Whatever it was, it was concealed somewhere behind the figures in the wayside shrines, and at the treacherous bends in mountain roads where flowers had been left to mark the spot where someone had come to grief. It was there in Innsbruck's Royal Church, in the Emperor Maximilian's incomplete tomb and the twenty-eight bronze statues surrounding it. It even lurked, masked in shadow, at the foot of mountains where the rock plunged into the cold waters of a lake.

*

I have never known the exact nature of the relationship between my mother and Hans. Very possibly there was nothing at all beyond friendship: that there certainly was, one that embraced Hans's whole family, with real warmth on all sides. The very idea that there was something more romantic between them might have been nothing more, or less, than my own unconscious hope that we could once again be a family of four, not three, with a father.

Whatever the truth of the situation, there is no denying my mother's delight in the company of Hans and his family. If I had to choose a single picture to illustrate her capacity for frank enjoyment, it would be the photo taken of her on one occasion at Gufidaun, with the Zingerles. She is wearing her *Dirndl* and sitting at a table, a glass of wine in her hand. Her head is thrown back and she is obviously hooting with laughter. *O fortuna*.

The only memento we brought back this time was a weather-house in the form of a chalet, with its two figures in traditional Austrian costume. I can't remember which one emerged to signal good weather, and which denoted bad.

It was a long time since we Norwood pupils had been issued with our free coronation mugs, and had wound along in a crocodile past the prison to St David's Church for a service of thanksgiving. At school the little wooden figures on the house points ladder had climbed up their rungs more than once. As models for optimism they were thus not ideal, since they always ended up by starting again at the bottom of the ladder, as if they had come up against a snake.

Beyond the little world of school, the city was renewing itself at last, buddleia giving way to brick, the bombsites replaced with smart new shops and a pedestrian precinct.

Now the spectre of Common Entrance loomed and, for some, the challenge inherent in the golden names on the school's honours board, of those who had won scholarships and exhibitions to public schools, some of greater renown than others. A sure sign that time was running out was that we were not impossibly far from Psalm 150. It was someone's bright idea – Robbie's, I suspect – that the boys in the upper forms should learn all the psalms by heart, one at a time. I remember him holding over us, with evident amusement, the threat of having to learn the whole of the seemingly endless Psalm 119 at one go.

The girls in the playground at Bishop Blackall's School, adjacent to Norwood, began to be of greater interest: we and they exchanged cheerful insults and remarks full of bravado, if nothing more, across the wire mesh between us. Another indication of time going on.

My name had been put down for King's School, Bruton, but Mummy decided that she would like me to follow in Uncle Basil's footsteps and go to Sherborne. Robbie took a dim view of this, pointing out that since I had not been entered for the school the only way I could try to get in was by sitting the scholarship exam, and he wasn't at all sure that I would get an award. Daddy would not have approved of either establishment: he told me years later that if he had had any say in it, which he evidently didn't, I would never have been sent to a private school, let alone as a boarder.

It must have been a good contest, the stubborn headmaster versus the stubborn mother. In the end Mummy prevailed. One consequence of this was the decision that I should offer Greek for the scholarship exam, in addition to the usual subjects. This meant that I would require intensive coaching. Every so often, therefore, I took a train down the Exe estuary, to sit in the study of the Reverend Addenbrooke, at Lympstone. This was good fun, or at least the journey was: and the currency of transgression being still bright, I got a kick from buying and eating chewing gum on the way. We were absolutely forbidden to have it at home. The sinfulness of it greatly enhanced the flavour of the sugary little white pillows. The cost of this enjoyment was, however, steep. I found the subject very difficult, and Latin didn't help. I sat there failing to understand very much at all, studying the specks of saliva which would gather at one corner of the genial Reverend Addenbrooke's lips, and gather again each time he wiped them away. He must have had a patience almost beyond his calling. Knowing the Greek alphabet came in handy, though, since it was used to denote candidates' performance in Sherborne's scholarship papers. Thanks to those lessons, when it came to it I was able to comprehend just how badly I had done in the Greek paper.

A welcome distraction from the classroom was the football team. After years of muddy thrashing about, I found myself included in the school's 1st XI, at inside left. It was reckoned to be a strong team that year, quite largely because of the presence of a very talented centre forward called Jan. He really was very much better than the rest of us, and scored goals with a regularity and casualness which excited enough admiration to overcome envy.

As the season went on, it began to look as if we might remain unbeaten. We played each of our opponents twice, once at home and once away, so that well before the end of the season it was possible to gauge the likely overall outcome. Given the highly individual nature of some of the pitches, home teams tended to have quite an advantage. The Norwood field had a slope sufficient to make the ball run away during one half, and to call for very hard uphill booting of it for the other. All matches were contested very vigorously, not only those against our Exeter rivals Bramdean, but also St Peter's at Lympstone, Ravenswood, in the hinterland north of Tiverton, and Montpellier, a school in Paignton. What many of these occasions had in common was mud and rain, and terrible goal-mouth skirmishes in the mire. We knew from Robbie's Latin lessons that the legionaries habitually retired to winter quarters, but for us the combat was unrelenting. You came off the field sodden and weighed down, with a considerable amount of the pitch wound round your studs.

We may have drawn one match, but I don't think we lost any. Robbie beamed, his smile released for once from its sardonic downturn. The only sadness was the prospect of not being able to play soccer at my next school, whichever one it turned out to be. There, I had been told, it would be rugby.

*

Mummy alerted me to the fact that a public school would have a person called a 'custos', whom I might encounter when I went up for the scholarship exam. It is unlikely that she would have known this herself, so I guess that Uncle Basil must have briefed her. Should I meet such a person, she said, I must be sure to tip him. Mummy was a great believer in tipping, not out of condescension and not particularly as a bonus for good service, but simply because she had been brought up to believe this was the thing to do. Tipping, in the world of her parents, described the status of the bestower as much as the diligence of the recipient.

I was grateful to her for this information since, on arrival at Sherborne, I was indeed met by a man wheeling a cranky old bicycle with a basket, in which he dumped my overnight bag. He took me to the sanatorium, where candidates were to stay, and I remembered to give him a tip, as my mother had instructed. He looked somewhat surprised, but pocketed the half-crown I had offered. The next occasion on which I saw him was a day or so later at the interview with the headmaster, R. W. Powell, where he was introduced to me as Dr Cundy, the school's senior maths master. Both of them enjoyed my look of startled embarrassment, and were very nice to me about it.

My other gaffe was to write about the wrong subject in the French essay paper. Choosing 'Toujours la politesse' as my subject, and carelessly misreading the title, I wrote about 'Toujours la politique'. Perhaps this was some kind of unwitting response to the teacher's assertion that in a scholarship exam the important thing was to show intelligence: if A was the question set and you couldn't write about it, write about B, he suggested. I had no intention of carrying out this bold but risky manoeuvre, but in the event I did.

Sherborne offered me an exhibition – the Baker Exhibition, though I never did find out who Baker was. Perhaps he or she set up the award to encourage those candidates who, not unlike the cavemen in the *Children's Encyclopaedia*, blundered about but meant well.

To have our father represented by his pictures on the wall was no substitute for having him there in the house, but Trinny and I were thrilled all the same that he gave us some of his work when we were young. The pictures speak for themselves, of course – but the temptation is that, given the relative sparseness of information about him, they might be read predominantly as illustrations of their maker's life. In the end, I found myself with more pictures than there had been meetings between us. They have accrued over the years, those given to me in childhood by Daddy joined by others – some bequeathed by his German relatives; three bought at a rare exhibition, in 1968; a couple found in the roof-space of his Somerset cottage after his death.

Daddy had not always had so little interest in exhibiting his pictures. In Germany, between 1929 and 1931, he had been represented in exhibitions in Düsseldorf, Cologne, Stuttgart, Berlin, Essen and Munich. After he had come to England, there were six exhibitions in as many years, among them one-man shows at two London venues; one of gouaches shown at the Storran Gallery (in 1935) and, three years later, an exhibition of eighteen oils and ten gouaches at the Calmann Gallery. The first of these attracted mildly favourable reviews in *The Times*, *The Observer* and *The Morning Post*, as well as a rather more considered review in *The New English Weekly* by the art critic Hugh Gordon Porteous, who noted that the artist had 'a curious preoccupation with the object, not merely with its visual aspect, but with its essence, subjectively apprehended'. Some of the pictures were, he thought, 'even allied in spirit with the work of Klee'.

Daddy does not seem to have kept track of his paintings in any systematic way: as far as I know, no complete list or catalogue exists. Nor do I know of any of his pictures having been acquired by public galleries, though a few found their way into the archive of the Rheinisches Museum in Cologne. It is not even clear that all of his pictures had titles: for those that did, they were always simple and brief. I cannot recall having talked with him much about art, either in general or in terms of his own work. Just as my mother treated art and literature as natural components of life, so with Daddy there was no sense of manifesto, just the doing of it. I have been slow to realise the value of this assumption which, between them, they handed on.

The range of what he did broadened over the years. He wove rugs, made earthernware vases and jugs, did silk-screen prints for curtains. At one point he took to growing tobacco. He also painted and fired tiles, a development that took him away from the representational and emphasised his talent for design and composition. Some were conceived as the tops of low tables. He painted inn signs for the brewer Ind Coope, whose best known brand, Double Diamond, I occasionally drank when I was older, by way of a distant salute. *Double Diamond works wonders!* ran the advertisement. Daddy also made a large tile mural for an inn called The Peacock, at Rowsley in Derbyshire. He usually made his own frames, too – of oak or cherry for the gouaches, and for the oils frames painted white, a number of them simple box frames.

The detailed chronology of his work is hard to figure out. The stylistic changes in his signature ought to offer a clue, but signatures (many of his were in faint pencil) can always be added later, and a number of the pictures are unsigned. Even when pictures are related in style and subject, and clearly painted at or about the same time, some are signed and others are not. As to the whereabouts of the pictures, they are scattered among family, friends and those who liked and bought his work.

What do the pictures themselves show, allowing for the fact that the thirty or so I have cannot be considered a complete record? Nearly all his pictures are representational, notwithstanding a brief period in the 1930s when he turned to emblematic landscapes somewhat in the manner of Paul Nash or de Chirico. The subjects to which he most frequently returns are boats, often seen clustered in a harbour or drawn up on a shore: sturdy fishing and sailing boats. He also painted still lifes, many with bottles and fruit; and increasingly, towards the end, studies of plants. Many of his pre-war paintings are gouaches, nearly all of the post-war ones, oils. The earliest gouaches date from a six-month visit Daddy had made to the Greek islands when he was twenty. Apparently he supported himself then by trading his work for food.

The first painting he gave me was a fair-sized watercolour of two stately three-masted schooners with banks of foresails and topsails, riding a calm pale sea flecked with the merest of ripples: no foam purls beneath the bowsprits. He gave Trinny a companion piece depicting a sloop with tan sails. But watercolours, like woodcuts and linocuts, accounted for only a little of his output: gouaches and oils were very much his main media. Probably the majority of his landscape paintings have their origins in the time he spent in Yugoslavia and Tossa de Mar, as well as Spanish towns such as Girona and Seville.

In all his work there is an attractive forthrightness which comes across in his use of line and colour, a quality sufficiently marked to be distinctively his own. Perhaps surprisingly, for a northerner, there is also an evident love of the Mediterranean world. The buildings and the boats in his pictures, for instance, even when they are not fully delineated, are unmistakably the kind to be found in, say, Spain, Greece or Italy, or on the Adriatic coast. In this it is possible to see the influence of his teacher in Cologne, Richard Seewald, who frequently travelled in the Mediterranean region and illustrated many books dealing with the area.

Humans and other creatures are almost wholly absent from Daddy's pictures. I know of only two small pictures, each of a toreador and bull, in which both are present. There is a late picture of two cockerels, but they are china ones. Two oils of a seated female nude are tentative, perhaps incomplete or abandoned. At Union Road there was also a maquette of a standing female nude. Well, not exactly standing, since it ended in a wooden base halfway down her thighs, but vertical anyway. I often wanted to ask Mummy whether she had been the model for this (and if not, who had been), but never quite had the courage to do so.

In some of the pre-war work, elements of the human figure are present as classical or mythical fragments: the torso of a fallen statue, the sculpted head of a woman, a mermaid, a man's stone head, a stone hand lightly clenched. The theatricality of these elements highlights a certain staginess, deployed elsewhere in his work to perhaps better effect, as in a gouache – one of his best – of the fish market at Barcelona. The foreground is occupied by a small sheaf of gaping fish laid out at a diagonal in the centre, with a prominent lemon yellow rowing boat on the left, seen stern on. At the top right hangs an oil lamp with a white mantle and topped with a wide brim of a shade. All these objects are seen in the context of a kind of proscenium arch made up of hanks of nets and canvas. The boat, pointing away, directs the viewer's eye towards a dark purple stretch of water and the lutulent outline of a building with a tower, its outlines bleeding into the night.

I don't think that, as children, we were ever struck by the absence of human figures in Daddy's pictures. Their presence was, after all, implied in the boats and buildings of his landscapes, or the fishnets drying in the sun. Among the pictures I have, the only exception is a set of six woodcuts, said to be illustrations for a book. Several of them show the head of a man, as well as the head and body of a siren or a mermaid: you sense that any accompanying narrative would be a mythical story of seduction. But one of the set shows a man sitting at his ease on a shore. Beside him, a knife lies next to a board on top of a quantity of paper, with bread, grapes, a lemon and a bottle. He is holding a pipe, and sits propped against a stout pillar of uncarved wood, one of three supporting a fruiting vine overhead. Seen through the frame of this arbour, a single boat rides a level sea, its one sail hanging from a spar as lifelessly as a curtain. Not only the posture of the seated figure, but his features as well, look very much like Daddy – but, eerily, as he was to become in later life rather than when these woodcuts must have been made. As for the setting, it seems a perfect encapsulation of the half-real, half-imagined south he loved so much. My half-sister has a similar picture entitled 'Picnic', showing a male figure reclining on a shore, with one boat beached and another on the water behind. Here, the picnic next to him consists of a watermelon, a baguette and a blue bottle labelled VIN.

Plants interested him more and more. In the later work the sisal to be seen in the foreground of many earlier pictures becomes increasingly prominent: in some instances it looks as aggressive as a triffid on the march. There are other bold paintings of plants seen close to – sunflowers, shepherd's purse, vervain.

The list of pictures in the 1968 exhibition enables a sounding of some sort. Of the twenty-six pictures on show (all of them oils), eight were of plants or flowers, six had to do with boats, while a further three were views of a seashore or an estuary. Five were of locations in Spain, including two relating to Tossa.

The very last picture Daddy painted is a return of sorts to the sea. It is a large, almost lurid oil painting of the remains of a boat on a beach. All the elements have been starkly rendered down, and the colours are blatant: the shore glares white and orange, the sky and sea present a glowering amalgam of mauve and grey. The boat itself, still just recognisable as such, is a charred black hulk, a disjointed rubble of strakes, transom and sternpost. Beyond it, nothing interrupts the featureless flow of the sea. The island which so often hovered in the background of his paintings has drifted out of sight altogether.

Only one of the paintings I have – an early one of a table with fruit, a sculpted hand and a partly visible sheet of music, on a dark green ground, is signed with the surname he had at birth.

*

Beyond and behind the paintings, the figure of my father remains hard to make out in the kind of familial detail you would expect, if not quite as indecipherable as his handwriting. He hardly ever wrote letters, but when he did it was like looking at a flatline graph with the very occasional upward flicker of life punctuating the onward horizontal flow. I always had to show or send his letters to Mummy, who would pencil in a plausible interpretation in her own entirely different hand – confident, open, beautifully legible. (But the number seven, so often credited with magic, offered common ground: both of my parents wrote it in the German style, with the spar of a small horizontal stroke crossing the upright.)

I never saw him weep, except with laughter, which was a wonderful thing to behold. Whenever I managed to induce those tears in him, I felt proud of being able to do so and, really, closer to him than at any other time. I also never saw him ill at ease with himself: he was, as the French say, *bien dans sa peau*. I remember him touching once on the subject of his first marriage, regretting it had come to grief and saying he was still very fond of Mummy. Certainly the two of them had affinities in addition to their love of art, in particular an appetite for travel, a dislike of pretentiousness and a keen eye for the absurd. He also enjoyed driving, as she did, and it isn't hard to imagine the fun they must have had from their pre-war touring abroad. In other respects there were clear differences, whether in his generally bolder, less inhibited approach to things, or his delight in cooking. I retain a memory of him preparing a cucumber salad, with a relish moderated only by his fear that it might somehow be too indigestible for me, and then lead to my returning home unwell, something that he either pretended to dread or really did: it wasn't easy to tell from his comic manner. When it came to it, it was he who over-indulged and suffered from stomach-ache: or said he did. In any case, food, drink and cigars were indispensable pleasures to him. The very last letter I

151

had from him, on my way back from Kenya, asked me to buy him 'some of those damn cheap cigars' when the boat called at Las Palmas. One way or another, he seemed to have the ambiguous gift of living in the present, the tense commandeered to a greater or lesser extent by many who vanish before their time. He took things as they came.

There was an element of mildly anarchic clowning in his character which was very appealing to children. I once saw him hamming it up on an open-air dance floor in Tossa, draping himself round the neck of his dancing partner, the habitual cigar between his lips and the ash on it getting ever longer, his eyes half-closed to keep out the smoke.

His love of drink produced a variety of effects. Also in Tossa, he gave a drinks party to which he invited two Americans. For some reason he had a generic dislike of that nation, expressed for the purposes of this occasion in a decision to spike a canvas chair in which he would then invite one of them, whom he considered much too pleased with himself, to sit down. The American duly sat down, the chair duly collapsed under him. But such was the good humour of the victim that it was Daddy who ended up feeling that a trick had been played on him. Deep in the night, long after the guests had gone home, I heard him angrily addressing the moon, in his strongly accented English: 'The trouble with these Americans, they think they are the cat's whiskers! You take away the whiskers, and you still have the damn cat.'

Daddy was the subject of the only other recurrent childhood dream which I can recall, in addition to the one that led to me being sent away. The setting was always the same: a deserted road bridge over a river, at night. Unblinking lights were set high above the bridge's arched back, with tall buildings vaguely in the background. It might have been a frontier zone. All this was seen as if from a window, at some distance.

Initially, only silence and an uncertain sense of anticipation. Enter a man in an overcoat with the belt hanging loose. He was leaning slightly to one side to offset the weight of the suitcase he was carrying. I knew this to be my father, even though I could not see his face clearly, just as I knew that the suitcase was stuffed with papers. A large old case, obviously heavy, needing to be tugged at like a recalcitrant animal. Every so often one of its corners banged into his legs. Close to the centre of the bridge he stopped, put down the case, rubbed and flexed the arm which had been carrying it. Then he leant on the parapet and gazed out over the dark twisting current. A car crossed the bridge behind him and vanished down the far slope. The overhead lights shone on. His breath looped in front of him, a blank speech balloon. He bent down, picked up the case with both hands and swung it up onto the parapet. It slithered there clumsily and, whether by design or accident, toppled into the darkness. Daddy leant forward and peered down, before crossing to the other side of the bridge to look down again at the viscous flow. Then he turned away and walked slowly on, head down, and soon was out of sight.

*

Increasingly, in growing up, I was aware of the ambivalence which underlay my feelings about my father. Circumstances had arranged that I was to be the only male in a household of three people, just as Daddy became in his second marriage. If this could be difficult, it also had its license. On the few occasions that we saw one another, he and I always got on extremely well: but what if we had lived under the same roof? We might have scrapped furiously, or even fallen out completely. The knowledge of this possibility, a kind of pre-emptive guilt (or a failure of nerve, perhaps) which I suspect we shared even though we never discussed it, kept our relationship on the casual level of occasional drinking partners.

Of course the question is, in a sense, a false one – if Daddy had always been there the kaleidoscope would no doubt have been shaken into different patterns, but patterns all the same. More pertinent is the question of how his absence affected Trinny. Not only in temperament and interests, but also in the close dualities of mother–son, father–daughter, it was she who had to face the consequences of the divorce most directly, the isolation of her position deepened by the limited ground that she and Mummy had in common. Her rare meetings with her father must have involved a terribly anxious and intense wish for closeness, sufficient to make the goal virtually unreachable for either of them. When we were small, and before words got in the way, it was easier: Daddy was naturally affectionate, and cuddling did it.

It seemed a strange place to be. Though it was summer, it was cold and a louring sky threatened rain. The air smelt strongly of something that we soon identified as burning peat, the pungent smell that Trinny and I had got to know only too well from inhaling it years before, under the intimate cover of a teacloth.

Even the name of the place sounded unsettled: Stornaway. Not as unsettled, though, as the water which we had crossed overnight from Kyle of Lochalsh.

The teacher had written to Mummy earlier in the year, asking whether we would like to join him for three weeks in Scotland, where he often went for his holiday. The four of us would drive up the west coast, then over to Inverness and back via Edinburgh. Mummy accepted. Trinny and I had never been to Scotland before, and neither had she. It would be an education, she said.

The journey north was characterised by two regular features – rain and double beds. We would drive till about four o'clock, then start to look for a bed and breakfast. The aim was to take two double rooms: one for Trinny and Mummy, one for the teacher and me. Once or twice we had no luck, and ended up at as cheap a hotel as we could find.

Each day we would have a picnic lunch, then a high tea at some café or other. There wasn't much to do in the evenings. On the rare occasions when the weather was reasonable, we might go for a walk: otherwise, we would turn in early. A diversion of a kind occurred at Kendal, where the crown came off one of Trinny's front teeth and, since the nerve was exposed painfully, a dentist had to be found.

I didn't like sharing a room with the teacher, or the fact that the bed was a double one. Just once we had a room with a double and a single bed, but apparently the single bed was not made up. I tried to get into my pyjamas while he was in the bathroom or, if he wasn't, to get undressed with the greatest possible privacy.

Mummy wrote a jocular account of the journey as we went along, beginning with her and Trinny, who had been at a family wedding in London, taking a train to Gloucester to meet me and the teacher. On the way she and Trinny must have talked about us. They hoped, she wrote, that we were behaving ourselves and that the teacher was not hugging or walloping me.

Even forty-five years on, I find those words hard to comprehend. The trouble was that hugging and walloping were exactly what the teacher liked. We would get into bed and sooner or later, with or without the pretext of some kind of game, it would begin: more walloping than hugging, as it happened.

If my mother knew – and even before the journey had started – what was going on, how could she let it go on happening? And how did she know, anyway? I don't recall anything like that taking place before the Scottish holiday, but perhaps it had and she was wise to it somehow. Presumably, given that she could refer to it so jokily, she thought it was just horseplay. And so it was, in a way. Though there were times when the teacher was evidently in a state of some excitement, my mother's description remained exact: there was never anything more. As after the night in the tent with my school friend, nothing was ever said in the morning. The whole business made me feel intensely ill at ease.

The other puzzle, of course, is why I didn't tell my mother. Here I think I can discern a whole welter of confused thoughts and motives: pride, shame, a desire to protect Mummy's feelings and even those of the teacher. Because it seemed to me, and still does, that there was a terrific struggle going on in him. What does that prayer say, or some part of someone's liturgy? 'The good that we would, we do not; the evil that we would not, we do'. Or words to that effect. *Not that it worries me*, Mummy confided to her journal, *sharing a bed with Trinny*.

The situation was not simple. Here was a man who had shown me friendship and generosity, who had given me a hint of what it might have been like to have a father around – and who had taught me a lot. I was grateful to him for all that. And there was the holiday itself to think of: to say something would surely have been to wreck it. But there was also the misery of not telling anyone – like living in a house alone, with heavy curtains drawn all the bright day long.

None of this should be taken for an apologia or a justification. As has been said, 'tout comprendre, c'est tout comprendre'. I suppose another charitable view would be that we are all fallible, but some people make the wrong mistakes.

*

At Stornaway Trinny and Mummy stayed at a hotel, while the teacher and I were put up by a friend of his, a minister, who was waiting for us at the quayside and took us off to the manse to meet his wife and children. It seemed that the

157

teacher had friends, as well as cousins, dispersed over Scotland from Glasgow to Montrose and all round the houses in between. Some of these friends had been in the army with him during the war, or at some other time had been involved with the Scouts, like him. More than once we went, just the two of us, to meet one of them. I thought nothing of it at the time but, looking back, wonder whether I was being shown off as a trophy. I'd like to think not.

The holiday went on and we saw a lot, both before and after the Stornaway visit: Loch Ness, Urquhart Castle (where the teacher said that his ancestors had lived), Oban, Staffa, Glencoe. On Iona the teacher bought me a small cross of moss agate, on an agate base.

The weather continued to be changeable, and perhaps everyone began to feel that three weeks could be a long time. It was noticeable that in the latter stages there seemed more frequently to be cousins or friends for the teacher to go off and see on his own. When we got to Edinburgh, during the final week of the Festival, like a homing pigeon released from its crate Mummy went to the Usher Hall and got the three of us tickets for a concert featuring the Vienna Boys' Choir and members of the Vienna Philharmonic.

*

The friendship went on for a time. Once, I was spending a night at the teacher's house. I always stayed in a room down the corridor from his own bedroom, which I had never entered. Looking for him in the morning one day, I knocked at his door and he called to me to come in.

Two of the walls were covered with photographs, all of them of boys about my own age. I felt at a complete loss – amazed, humiliated.

'Can you find yourself?' he asked pleasantly.

Later, he removed every one of those pictures. Nothing remained but the ghosts of them, pale rectangles, squares and ovals imprinted on the darker wallpaper where they had hung.

In the lanes the hedgerows had moved in, narrowing the roadway with flowers and grasses. Soon everything would begin to look a bit exhausted, the gloss of the leaves covered with a film of dust. Soon it would be time to go.

It was a warm summer evening and the windows of the van were wound down. I was sitting next to Stuart, on the way to one village hall or another.

'Well now,' he said and cleared his throat. Well now, I would be going away soon, wasn't that right. Yes, and boarding for the first time. A pause. 'Yes,' I said, which he then repeated. He gazed out of the window as if trying to remember what it was he had been going to say. Then he looked out through the windscreen again.

The manner was familiar, but I hadn't quite seen him in this role before. It was beginning to sound a bit important, if not portentous: but then I knew this would be the last time I saw him before I went off to Sherborne, so perhaps it was something to do with that.

There were various false starts, and a sentence beginning 'Your mother …' which trailed off into silence: and he may well have taken refuge in an anecdote. For an awful moment I thought there was going to be some dreadful inquest relating to the Scottish holiday. Finally, however, it came out that my mother had asked him to have a word with me about boarding school life. I'm not at all sure that the script he finally delivered was one which would have met with official approval. 'You see, old man, it might be that …'. His message was actually very simple: boys of about my age often took an interest in each other, and it might even be expressed physically, and I shouldn't worry about that, it wasn't necessarily something to feel guilty about, especially at a boarding school where everyone was cooped up together. He said all this very gently, and I loved him for it.

It was my turn to gaze out. I think I mumbled that I understood and Stuart, evidently relieved to have completed his mission, embarked on a story about the Marx Brothers.

*

Soon it would be time. Everything had been bought, name-tapes sewn on, the long clothing lists ticked. I had even practised the use of collar studs, bending the flyaway detached collar into place, after first folding my tie into it. The large blue trunk stood ready to be packed – not the old kind bound with strips of varnished wood, but really a large blue composition suitcase. As well as my name in white paint, it had a small coloured transfer of a globe, and the brand name: *Globetrotter*. That should see me safely as far as Dorset. Beside it stood a traditional wooden tuck-box, also with my name painted on it, in thick black letters. All the heavy stuff was due to be sent ahead, Passenger Luggage in Advance.

For Trinny, the business of leaving home had become a routine. For me, it was horribly new. It induced, along with a certain excitement, a hollow of anticipatory dread in the pit of my stomach.

*

It was time. At Central Station, where almost exactly ten years before Daddy had become entangled in the dog's lead, I stood on the platform with my overnight bag.

161

The dark grey herring-bone suit, bought with room to allow for growing, hung loosely on me. The collar, stud and tie arrangement, also too big, felt very odd. I had the feeling that I was about to come apart.

Ahead of me, a world still predicated largely on pre-war values and assumptions; and a flight of worn stone stairs leading up to the school chapel. *Tooshk, tooshk* go the boys' feet each morning, as they climb up past the illuminated Books of Remembrance. *Tooshk, tooshk*, in the autumn of Suez.

The train drew in. All too soon we were bowling along through open country. Looking out over the fields, I could see that the leaves on the trees were turning, but had not yet started to fall.

Death, whenever and however it arrives, gives shape of a kind to any life. It sets in motion the process by which the past is invented. Fictile, we become fiction. If you disbelieve what believers say, everyone dies happily or unhappily ever after.

There are films which know how to do it. Before or after the end credits, on a black ground and with no accompanying sound, a paragraph or so tells the audience what has become of the characters.

Stuart succumbed to liver cancer at the age of sixty. I remember going to see him before he died. He tried to sit up, and grasped at me. 'I'd give anything for just two more years,' he said. Today his son Nicholas runs the Exeter Film Society.

The teacher took to spending his holidays in the Philippines in later life. He was 'gathered in', as a friend used to describe it euphemistically, some years ago, and is buried in the grave-yard of the church he had done so much to sustain.

Hans, a bachelor for many years, in the end married an old friend, Martha Fischer. After she died of cancer, he committed suicide.

Daddy, who had been looking forward to his imminent retirement from the art school in Burton-on-Trent, suffered a fatal heart attack one January night. I learned of his death on my way back from Kenya, where I had been teaching. I rang my mother from Paris, as we had agreed I would, and she told me. He was sixty-two. His father, Heinrich, had died of heart disease at the age of fifty-nine. It was a very strange experience to carry the knowledge of my father's death with me as the train continued north-westwards under a bright, almost full moon, passing more than once by large war cemeteries: all those multiples of loss marked plus.

One of Daddy's ambitions for his retirement had been to visit Japan: he had long been interested in Japanese art and house design. Another had been for us to see more of each other. He is buried in West Somerset, where he had reno-vated a tiny cottage. After his death, I bought this cottage from my stepmother Dolores. She moved a few miles away to be with her two sisters, both of whom she outlived. She died shortly before the new millennium.

Mummy, after nearly a quarter of a century on her own, married her hairdresser, 'Tommy' Thompson. He had been an R.A.F. bomb-loader during the war: a fine irony. They had ten or so happy years together, until his death. She herself had to stop playing tennis at the age of eighty, when she broke her foot. She took to swimming instead, forgetting that she had hardly ever mastered the skill. When she floundered, whoever came to her aid was invited back for coffee – made, no doubt, by the Viennese method. She died in 2000, at the age of eighty-nine. Her ashes joined Tommy's in the church-yard at Hurley, in Berkshire, where she had lived for over thirty years after leaving Exeter in 1961.

Peggy, Mummy's twin, outlived her husband by many years, suffered increasingly from arthritis, which she defied with real stoicism, and ended her days in a home in Kent, at the age of eighty-two. She had easily the most memorable funeral of anyone in the family. The priest appeared to be drunk, but turned out to have had a stroke that had left him with impaired speech. Most unforgettable of all was his address, which began ringingly: 'Why, I'm three-quarters dead; some of you look as if you're half-dead – but (*indicating the coffin*) Peggy there, why, Peggy is *completely* dead. No more washing up for Peggy!'

Trinny trained as a Margaret Morris Movement dancing teacher, then did a Constance Spry floristry course and worked for a time in a London florist's close to Victoria Station. She then completed a nursery nurse's course and worked in this field before meeting and marrying David, a mechanical engineer who turned to photography. They live in Oxford.

My half-sister Amata lives in Wales with her second husband Rodney. A jig and tool designer, he is also a skilled sailor who built his own boat in Australia and sailed it to England. They have two children, John and Debbie. They still have the boat and sail frequently.

As for my father's German relatives, it had always been Daddy's intention to take me to meet them. In the event, I first met two of them – his half-brother Wolfgang and Lotte, his wife – at Daddy's funeral. Since then I have got to know others in the German family, and contact is infrequent but real. Among them I think especially of Hildegard, another of Daddy's half-siblings, and my cousin Thomas, a documentary film producer. Daddy had talked of both of them with great affection. Hildegard, who became a Protestant nun and worked as a children's psychiatric nurse, was born with a distortion of the features which looked a bit like Bell's palsy: she was also short and rather lame. I learned only after her death that her father had implored the nuns to take her in. Presumably, with the rise of Hitler, this was her best hope of safety.

On one occasion Wolfgang and Lotte presented me with a

set of delicate silver teaspoons engraved with the initials of my paternal grandmother, Frieda, whom I had never known. They were apologetic about the fact that there were only five, of the original set of six. This struck me as entirely appropriate, in keeping with that *Leitmotif* of absence which permeates my perception of my father: one spoon short of a family. A number of years later other German relatives, ignorant of the earlier gift, presented me with an identical set of teaspoons, likewise engraved with my grandmother's initials. They regretted, however, that there were only five …

Edgerton Park is a school no longer, but sheltered accommodation; Norwood is an old people's home. Somewhere inside hangs a picture of the 1956 1st XI football team, which someone thought would add a nice historical touch. Exeter City, meanwhile, after a time in the wilderness has been promoted twice in succession and at the time of writing is in League One – the equivalent of the Third Division in which it found itself half a century ago.

The city itself, or at any rate a large chunk of the centre, was recently once again reduced to rubble: but this time by ball and chain rather than bombs. The original pedestrian precinct of Princesshay has gone, replaced by a shiny new version where, one or two items of public art notwithstanding, retail *über alles* seems to be the presiding spirit. Already some of the new shops have foundered in the current recession.

*

I, who as a child so longed to get back to London, returned to Exeter in 1975 after travels of my own. This was not premature nostalgia, but an acknowledgement that when it came to thinking of a good place to bring up a family, Exeter

– and Devon – would be hard to better. I have been there, or thereabouts, ever since.

Sometimes it is as if the history of the family over the years is a matter of adjustments, rather than radical departures. Perhaps this is in part genetic: there is a limit to what you can ask the genes not to do. When you superimpose my present surroundings and circumstances on those of my parents, it is not an exact match, but not far off: a bit blurred, rather like one of those newspaper pictures in which the infill of colours has not quite hit the target of the outlines. I live in Exeter, but in a different part of the city, one I did not know of when I was young. Our house has four floors, like Union Road, and is also aligned north–south. This house, too, has a basement at the front which becomes garden level at the back. Union Road had a total of forty-eight stairs: now we have forty-four.

A few hardy objects, more impervious to the changes effected by time than any photographs, live on – the large saucepan bought in Tottenham Court Road, the clockwork car from Austria (its hooter still in working order), the cowbell, my mother's workbox. The copy of *Cocolo*, the story about a donkey that I was given as a child, has also survived, even if its simple vision of a paradise that the young might intuit has long since become intertwined with a premonition of its unavailability. Yet, as if it were a slow-release infusion, the story of Cocolo has assumed the nature of a full and virtuous circle. Three years ago I opened those lemon yellow covers once again, for the benefit of three-year-old twins, and was able to observe with delight how the magic goes on. Or rather, round and round and round.

Like Daddy, I have been married twice. His first marriage lasted nearly twelve years, mine nearly sixteen. Matthew and

Erica, the children of that marriage, to Teresa, are now in their thirties. Grace and Rose, the twin daughters of my second marriage sixteen years ago, to Helen, are six. Here then, I think almost with relief, is a distinctive difference – Daddy's three children, my four. And then I recall my stillborn elder sister, with her blonde hair and blue eyes. As in the parable of the lost sheep, in the end it is always those who have absconded who present themselves to us most forcefully. Insubstantial, freed from time, they home to our imagination.